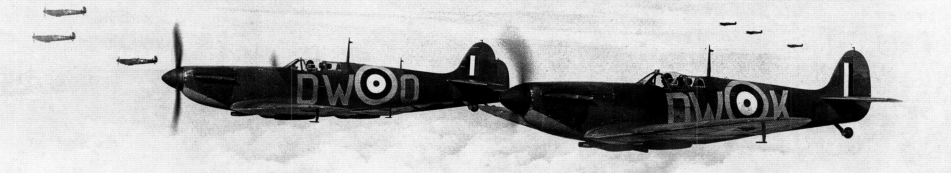

THE BATTLE OF
BRITAIN
EXPERIENCE

RICHARD OVERY

ANDRE
DEUTSCH

The Battle of Britain Experience is an official licensed product of the Royal Air Force. The Royal Air Force name and logo are trademarks of the Secretary of State for Defence and are used under licence.

This edition published in 2015 by ANDRÉ DEUTSCH
A division of the Carlton Publishing Group
20 Mortimer Street
London
W1T 3JW

ISBN 978 0 23300 452 5

ACKNOWLEDGMENTS

I am happy to acknowledge the extent to which this book has been a real team effort. The book's editor Gemma Maclagan has played a key part in getting the book together and keeping me on schedule. Russell Knowles, Sooky Choi and Steve Behan are responsible for the book's strong visual content and layout. Philip Parker and Peter Elliott have between them made sure that the history is as error-free as it can be and I am grateful to them for their scrupulous monitoring of the text and captions which has made this a better book.

CONTENTS

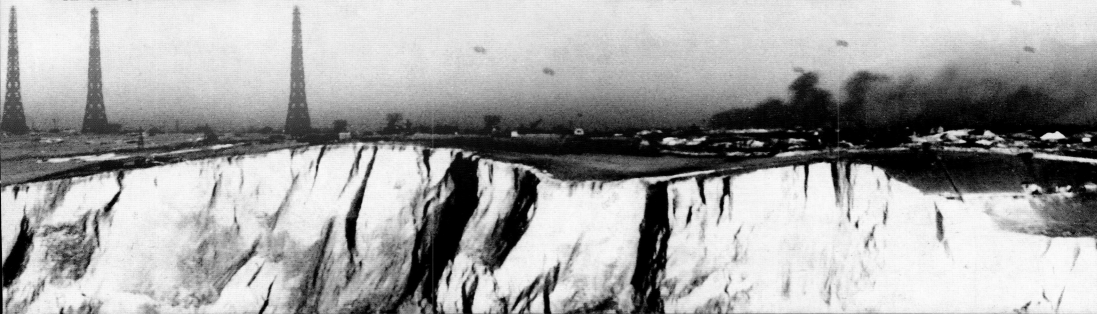

INTRODUCTION

No other battle in recent British history has been accorded the same status as the Battle of Britain, fought out over the skies of England in the summer and autumn of 1940 between the Royal Air Force and the German air force. The Battle followed on from the defeat of France in June 1940 and the expulsion of British forces from Continental Europe during the Dunkirk evacuation. The general expectation in Britain was of a German invasion at some point later in 1940. One way of ensuring that invasion might be postponed was to deny the German forces air superiority over southern England. The onus of achieving this fell on RAF Fighter Command. The failure of the German air force to eliminate British fighter defences played a critical part in persuading Hitler and his commanders that invasion was too risky. Hitler turned to planning war on the Soviet Union and the invasion threat disappeared.

Fighter Command was not the only reason that Hitler hesitated. Deteriorating weather, the threat of a powerful Royal Navy and the prospect of Bomber Command attacking the invasion beaches were all factors that contributed to the decision not to invade. But if Fighter Command had failed in its task of preventing the enemy

from dominating the skies of southern England, the outcome might have been different. This victory depended on many things, including the radar detection screen and high levels of aircraft output and pilot training. The many factors that affected the battle are explained in what follows. *The Battle of Britain Experience* is an invitation to explore the contest from many different angles. Each spread is rich in photographs and images from the time. There are also documents, maps and diaries that bring alive the sense of what it was like to endure that dangerous summer when it seemed that the German army, only 35 kilometres (22 miles) away across the Channel, might soon be tramping along English roads. The conflict certainly did not decide the war, which was won only five years later with powerful Allies at Britain's side. But it ensured that Britain, unlike much of the rest of Europe, did not have to come to terms with defeat and occupation. Like the destruction of the Spanish Armada 350 years before, the Battle of Britain has won a legendary place in Britain's island history.

Richard Overy

THE FIRST BATTLE OF BRITAIN

◎ 1917–18

When a German aircraft dropped a bomb on the port of Dover on 24 December 1914, it marked the first successful aerial attack on British soil. What followed was an intermittent series of attacks that increased in intensity by the middle of the First World War and petered out again after May 1918, six months before the war's end. In total, Britain was subjected to 51 attacks by German airships and 52 attacks by aircraft. This was on a small scale compared with the air battles of the Second World War, but the first Battle of Britain had important repercussions for the greater battle fought a generation later.

Air power was in its infancy in 1914 and the German decision to attack British targets from the air was based on unfounded speculation about the possible effects of aerial bombing. Most of the early attacks were undertaken by a few aircraft at a time and their impact was negligible. More dangerous was the German decision to undertake an offensive using airships, most of them the famous Zeppelins, that could carry large loads of bombs of varying calibre and which were at first virtually free to roam over British territory. The first airship attack was made on the night of 19–20 January 1915 and the last was mounted on 5–6 August 1918.

The threat posed by air attack was met at first by anti-aircraft guns stationed around vulnerable areas of the south-east of England and a limited number of fighter aircraft. The airships faced great difficulty in navigating successfully and unloaded their bombs when and where they could, but the efforts of the few defensive squadrons of the Royal Flying Corps were equally hampered by weather, slow speeds and a lack of suitable armament for destroying airships. Gradually, improved fighter aircraft managed to inflict losses on the Zeppelin fleet, but it was impossible to disguise the inadequacy of much of the early air defence effort. Yet by the end of 1916, the airships had dropped only 160 tons of bombs in two years. Neither side was in a position to do anything very decisive in the air war over Britain.

The situation changed with the German decision to mount a campaign in 1917 using heavy bombers. In the spring of 1917, the German high command was looking for a way to bring pressure to bear on Britain to pull out of the war. Alongside unrestricted submarine warfare they chose air attacks on London as a possible way of undermining popular war-willingness among both the public and politicians. The plan for a long-range bomber assault had been proposed by General Ernst von Hoeppner. Under his guidance the

ABOVE The wrecked German Zeppelin L15 lies in the Thames Estuary after being shot down on 31 March 1916 by the anti-aircraft battery at Purfleet. One crew member drowned and the rest were saved by a British destroyer.

MAJOR GENERAL SIR FREDERICK SYKES (1877–1954)

Appointed in April 1918 as the second chief of the air staff in succession to General Trenchard, Frederick Sykes had the task of nursing the fledgling RAF through its first year of existence. Sykes joined the army as a volunteer at the start of the South African War (1899–1902) and gained a full commission in 1901. In 1911, he learned to fly (his certificate was number 96), and in the pre-war years played an important part in the formation of the Royal Flying Corps. He became its first chief of staff in 1914 under General Sir David Henderson, but arguments with the army over the use of aircraft led to a posting to the Royal Naval Air Service in the Mediterranean. In 1918, he took up his role as chief of staff of the new RAF, a position he held until January 1919 when he went to the Paris peace talks as head of the British Air Section. He ran civil aviation in Britain for three years from 1919 and then entered parliament as a Conservative. He retired from politics in 1945.

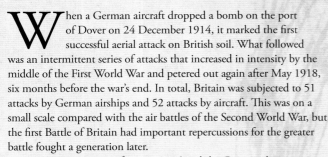

LEFT Damage caused to housing as a result of a German air raid. During 1917–18, 836 people were killed in attacks by German bomber aircraft and 1,982 injured.

BELOW RIGHT The burnt-out hull of a German airship that landed next to a cottage in southern England. Airships proved very vulnerable to poor weather conditions, and to enemy fire from fixed anti-aircraft artillery or from British fighter aircraft.

LEFT The early air attacks called for improvised civil defence. Here a car carries the "all clear" sign after an air alarm in October 1917, a month when south-east England was attacked both by Gotha bombers and by Zeppelins. By this stage of the war Britain was already using "black-outs" in threatened areas at night.

FIELD MARSHAL JAN SMUTS (1870–1950)

Jan Smuts played a key role in the creation of the Royal Air Force. A former Boer commander in the South African War, Smuts fought on the British side in Africa during the First World War before coming to London as a member of Lloyd George's war cabinet. It was in this capacity that he chaired the committee that organized the air defence of London in 1917 and recommended the formation of an independent air force. In August 1917, his proposals were accepted and, despite army opposition, a bill to create an air force passed through parliament in November. Smuts foresaw the widespread use of bomber aircraft in a new strategic role. After the war, he attended the Paris peace conference and then returned to a political career in South Africa where he became prime minister in 1919. He was a close friend and adviser of Churchill during the Second World War, and played a part in drafting the United Nations Charter in 1945.

so-called "England Squadron" was activated, commanded by Captain Ernst Brandenburg. Using heavy aircraft produced by the Gothaer Waggonfabrik – usually known as Gotha bombers – the squadron made its first attack in daylight on 25 May 1917 against the Kent port of Folkestone, killing 95 people. The public response was of panic and anger. When a raid on 12 June hit a school in the London district of Poplar, killing 18 children, the outrage was intense.

The bombing raids had an immediate effect. The London Air Defence area was set up and large numbers of anti-aircraft guns, searchlights and fighter aircraft made available. A war cabinet committee under General Smuts sat to consider possible solutions, and his recommendation of the creation of an independent air force paved the way for the foundation of the Royal Air Force, which was formally established on 1 April 1918 with a strength of 165,000 men. The air defence system was overhauled by Brigadier General Edward Ashmore so that proper warning could be given. By the end of the war, London was defended by 304 guns, 415 searchlights and 11 fighter squadrons of 24 aircraft each. The result in autumn 1917 was to force the German bombers to shift to night raids, which made accurate bombing impossible. British night-fighters began to impose heavier losses on the attacking force and by May 1918 the German offensive came to an end. The 103 attacks had resulted in 1,400 deaths and 3,400 serious injuries. The strategic result was in the long run disastrous for the German side. Britain remained in the war but also came to understand the nature and limitations of air defence. In 1940 Britain would be much better prepared for an air assault than it had been in 1917.

BELOW Soldiers and onlookers surround a crashed German Gotha bomber in Kent. In total, 54 of the bombers were lost through enemy action or accidents. One was forced to land in neutral Holland.

AIR DEFENCE BETWEEN THE WARS

ABOVE RIGHT A formation of Armstrong-Whitworth Siskin aircraft from 41 Squadron RAF in flight. The single-seat biplane fighter was designed by the motor company Siddeley Deasy in 1919 but was taken over by Armstrong-Whitworth two years later. It was noted for its high aerobatic performance and was a favourite at air displays. It was retired from service in 1932.

LEFT An aerial view of the Hendon Air Display, held annually in the 1930s at the RAF airfield in north London. The display shows new aircraft models on show to the public.

BELOW An event at the Hendon Air Display in 1928. A favourite feature was to stage a mock bomb attack on a reconstructed African or Arab village, a form of combat known in British Empire conflicts as "air policing".

The development of the RAF during the interwar years suffered from an evident contradiction. On the one hand, most leading airmen and air theorists assumed that air power was most effective when used in an offensive bombing role. On the other, Britain's evident vulnerability to air attack, demonstrated during the First World War, made the development of an effective air defence against enemy bombing imperative. For much of the interwar period, it was assumed that the balance of advantage lay with the attacking bomber aircraft. The difference in performance between fighters and bombers was too small to give fighters much chance of getting into the air, finding the enemy and shooting them down. The general view was that possession of a bomber force which could threaten a potential enemy, a posture that was called deterrence, would be sufficient defence against attack. Not until the mid-1930s was this view finally challenged by the development of a sophisticated air defence system in the United Kingdom, the only one of its kind in existence when war broke out in 1939.

In 1925, the RAF was reorganized under the title Air Defence of Great Britain. The bomber squadrons were concentrated on airfields in the central and southern areas of the country, and the fighters in a narrow belt to the south of London. For much of the next 10 years the only likely enemy was considered to be France and aircraft were deployed to meet that implausible threat. After 1933, the rise of Hitler's Germany created a menace which the existing ADGB organization was inadequate to face. In 1936, the ADGB was abolished and replaced with separate functional commands – Bomber Command, Fighter Command and Coastal Command. The forces were then redistributed to meet the more likely German challenge. Bomber bases were shifted to eastern England, in Yorkshire, East Anglia and Lincolnshire, where beforehand there had been only a single RAF base. Fighter aircraft were redeployed to cover the whole area of southern and eastern England, from Southampton to Newcastle. By 1939, there were 138 airfields instead of the 52 available five years

STANLEY BALDWIN (1867–1947)

The Conservative politician Stanley Baldwin is perhaps best remembered for his remark made in the House of Commons on 10 November 1932 that "the bomber will always get through". His view of future air war as something that would utterly destroy civilization played an important part in shaping popular fears of bombing during the 1930s. He was three times prime minister between 1923 and 1937. Under the National Government, set up in 1931, he was effectively deputy prime minister with the title of Lord President of the Council. It was during this period that he played a part in helping to set up the Disarmament Conference in Geneva and it was partly from the hope that he could achieve a real measure of disarmament in the air that he embarked on his scaremongering campaign. When he became prime minister in 1935, he oversaw the early stages of British rearmament, despite his lasting commitment to appeasement, seeing it as a better way to avoid the prospect of a terrible war.

before. Fighter Command was supplemented by a chain of radar stations, developed between 1936 and 1939 to give early warning of approaching aircraft, and by ground observers to track incoming aircraft. From 1936 onwards, under pressure from the government, the RAF also shifted the balance between bomber and fighter production, which had previously favoured offensive aircraft. By the outbreak of war, the RAF was structured both to defend against an enemy air offensive and to mount an offensive against the same enemy on the untested assumption that their opponent's defence against bombing would be less adequate than the RAF's own.

The government was also aware that the threat of bombing created widespread public alarm. Alongside the advent of an active air defence came developments in ground defences and civil defence. Anti-aircraft artillery had been used in the First World War and although its effectiveness was questionable, the presence of guns helped to reassure the local population. In 1937, an Ideal Plan was formulated for a system of guns, searchlights and barrage balloons. By 1939, only 570 heavy guns had been made available out of a planned 1,264, but much of the shortfall was made good in the first nine months of the war.

More important for public morale were civil defence preparations.

These had been almost non-existent when bombing began in the First World War. In 1924, the government set up an Air Raid Precautions Sub-Committee, run by the Home Office, whose task was to plan and prepare for possible bomb attack. During the 1930s these plans were finally given real substance. In 1937, a comprehensive Air Raid Precautions law was introduced, requiring local authorities to establish a nationwide ARP structure, to be organized and supervised by Regional ARP Commissioners. Huge numbers of volunteers came forward to act as air raid wardens and emergency personnel. By 1940, there were 828,000, including 108,000 full-time civil defence workers. Local councils were obliged to begin a programme of air-raid shelter construction and, together with the police, to organize exercises in blacking out towns. By 1939, Britain was the only country to distribute a gas mask to every man, woman and child (on the assumption that a ruthless enemy was almost certain to use gas or germ warfare in the event of war). A comprehensive evacuation scheme was prepared for children and mothers, to come into force as soon as war was declared. The system was far from complete when war did eventually break out, but it was sufficiently advanced to provide a measure of warning and shelter to most of the threatened population.

BELOW LEFT Two young children try out the new respirators (gas masks) distributed to almost everyone in Britain during 1939 and 1940. Beside the standard adult mask was a special respirator for babies and the small children's mask illustrated here.

BELOW Workmen assigned to air raid precautions work dig trenches in London's Hyde Park on 28 September 1938. That day the British public waited to hear if war over Czechoslovakia had been averted. Fear of bombing dominated public anxieties during the crisis which ended with the Munich agreement, signed two days later.

AIR CHIEF MARSHAL SIR CYRIL NEWALL (1886–1963)

The most important post in the RAF during the Battle of Britain was held by the chief of the air staff Cyril Newall. He began his military career in the army in 1905, learned to fly in 1911, and served in the Royal Flying Corps during the First World War, reaching the rank of brigadier general. In 1917 he was assigned to organize an aircraft wing for retaliatory raids on Germany and he became convinced that bombing could have serious strategic effects. He became deputy chief of the air staff between 1926 and 1931 and chief of the air staff in 1937. He played an important part in expanding the pre-war RAF, both its defensive capability and the power to hit back with heavy bombers. He protected the fighter force from Churchill's demands for more aircraft in the Battle of France, and remained in office until the end of October 1940, with that battle almost over. He became governor general of New Zealand until 1946.

FIGHTER COMMAND

◎ 1940

Fighter Command was only four years old when the Battle of Britain began. It formally came into existence on 14 July 1936 when the RAF was divided into four separate commands – Fighter, Coastal, Bomber and Training. The new force was placed under the command of Air Marshal Hugh Dowding and its headquarters sited at Bentley Priory on the outskirts of London. Although fighter squadrons had existed in the old air defence system, Dowding faced the remarkable challenge of having to create an entirely new and effective fighting organization in a matter of a few years.

The force was divided into a number of groups to defend particular geographical areas, and each group contained a number of sector stations where the operational aircraft were based. The south-east of England was defended by 11 Group; the Midlands and East Anglia by 12 Group; and the north and north-east of England were the

responsibility of 13 Group. In response to the threat to Britain's ports and shipping, 10 Group was set up in July 1940 to defend the west and south-west. Eventually 14 Group and 9 Group were formed to protect Scotland and the north-west, particularly against attacks on naval shipping. The groups could collaborate and offer mutual support, but the operational commanders were responsible only for the sector aircraft covered by the territory of their group.

The heart of the new Command was the system of operational control and communication which allowed information on raids supplied by radar and visual observation to be fed back to Fighter Command headquarters and then passed on to the operational groups and sector stations. The central control of the fighter defence force made success possible in the Battle of Britain. Operations rooms were set up at Bentley Priory and at the Group headquarters. Here special

ABOVE A trainee RAF pilot using a Link trainer in 1940. Fighter Command expanded its training programme as rapidly as possible after the outbreak of war to provide around 1,200 pilots available for operations for most of the battle.

BELOW Barrage balloons being hoisted above the Thames from river barges. The balloon screen was partly to allay public fears and partly to force enemy aircraft to fly higher or risk an accident. On the first day of the war, 624 balloons were erected around the vulnerable target areas.

BENTLEY PRIORY

The command headquarters of Fighter Command was based in the eighteenth-century country house of Bentley Priory in Stanmore, Middlesex. The house began life as an aristocrat's estate, but by the late Victorian age it was a hotel, and then briefly a girls' boarding school. The estate was bought by the RAF in 1926 and was originally the site of RAF Training Command. In the summer of 1936, the newly created Fighter Command moved its headquarters to the Priory from Uxbridge. Under its first commander-in-chief, Hugh Dowding, the Priory was modified to incorporate an operations room and filter room to allow close central command over the whole fighter force. The Observer Corps also moved to Bentley Priory and the Anti-Aircraft Command was stationed nearby. An underground operations block was added in early 1940 and was in use by March of that year, but the headquarters suffered almost no bomb damage throughout the war. The Priory was finally abandoned by the RAF in May 2008.

AIR COMMODORE ALFRED WARRINGTON-MORRIS (1883–1962)

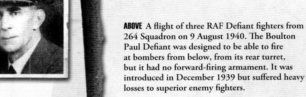

Alfred Warrington-Morris was the second commandant of the Observer Corps attached to Fighter Command. He saw service throughout the Battle of Britain. Morris joined the Royal Navy in 1899, rising to the rank of commander in the Royal Naval Air Service during the First World War. In 1918 he joined the Royal Flying Corps and by 1919 became a wing commander in the RAF. He was an air commodore and commandant of the RAF Signals Branch at his retirement in 1934. He was then appointed deputy commandant of the new Observer Corps, and became its commandant in April 1936. He helped transfer the Corps to Fighter Command's control and was still commandant when the title "Royal" was added and the Corps became a uniformed part of the RAF in 1942. He finally retired from RAF duties in 1944.

ABOVE A flight of three RAF Defiant fighters from 264 Squadron on 9 August 1940. The Boulton Paul Defiant was designed to be able to fire at bombers from below, from its rear turret, but it had no forward-firing armament. It was introduced in December 1939 but suffered heavy losses to superior enemy fighters.

RIGHT Two images show the importance of communication at the heart of the Fighter Command organization. **Top**: the filter room at Fighter Command headquarters at Bentley Priory where information from radar stations and the Observer Corps were marked on a large tabletop operations map. **Bottom**: a schematic diagram of the whole structure of Fighter Command communication in 1940.

map rooms were created which allowed the accurate plotting of incoming enemy aircraft and of the operations of the fighter forces scrambled to intercept them. Communication was by phone line, maintained by Post Office engineers. The information was taken from a chain of radar stations around the coast and from the men and women of the Observer Corps, staffed by volunteers to provide detailed information from ground observation of the direction and number of enemy aircraft. The corps came directly under Dowding's command and by 1940 comprised some 30,000 full-time and part-time members, organized in 32 groups, each one made up of approximately 50 observer posts.

In addition to the Fighter stations and the Observer Corps, Dowding also acquired control over the Balloon Command set up under Air Vice Marshal Owen Boyd in November 1938 and the Army's Anti-Aircraft Command, led by Lieutenant General Frederick Pile, a personal friend of Dowding. His command headquarters was posted to Bentley Priory on 28 July 1939 and the two men had regular discussions day after day on defence priorities

and tactics. The opposition offered by Fighter Command to the Luftwaffe in 1940 was greatly strengthened by the close integration of the fighter force with other forms of static defence.

The force that Dowding led was slowly converted from obsolete biplanes to the fast monoplane Hurricane and Spitfire fighters which became the mainstay of the Command. At the outbreak of war there were 35 fighter squadrons, but only 22 had the modern aircraft. By June 1940 Dowding had 48 squadrons – with more in the process of formation – equipped almost entirely with the latest models. The expansion in 1939–40 was aided greatly by mobilizing the Auxiliary Air Force (the air equivalent of the Territorial Army), which manned 14 squadrons during the battle, and by using the almost 5,000 men trained in the RAF Volunteer Reserve scheme (begun in April 1937 to train pilots in peacetime). The Reserve supplied almost one-third of the pilots who fought in the Battle of Britain. By the summer of 1940, poised to await the German assault, Fighter Command was one of the best-equipped and most efficient elements of Britain's armed forces.

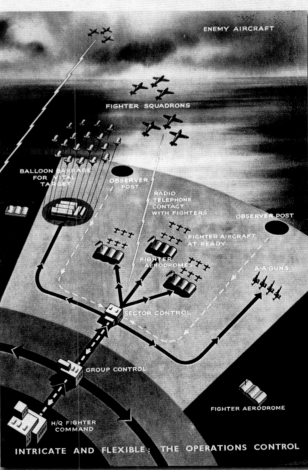

INTRICATE AND FLEXIBLE: THE OPERATIONS CONTROL

THE LUFTWAFFE

◎ 1940

The German air force was reborn in March 1935 when Hitler formally announced that Germany was rearming in defiance of the Treaty of Versailles. The first German air force was abolished in 1919 when the terms of the Treaty denied Germany any military aircraft or an organized air force. During the 1920s, the German army kept abreast of current aviation developments and, following agreements in 1922 and 1926 with the Soviet Union, German pilots were given facilities at Soviet air bases to try out new aircraft. The Defence Ministry had an office of air affairs and when Hitler came to power in January 1933, it was hoped that this could form the nucleus for secret air rearmament.

Hitler's close political ally, Hermann Goering, former commander of the Richthofen squadron at the end of the Great War, was unwilling to allow the army to create a new air force. He was appointed Air Minister in Hitler's government, and undertook the task of reviving a

ABOVE A German pilot and crew in the cockpit of a German bomber in September 1939. German air personnel were highly trained and their aircraft among the most technically sophisticated in the world.

military aviation industry and secretly recruiting and training a new generation of pilots. Many of those who joined the secret air force had had experience in the numerous flying and gliding clubs set up in Germany in the 1920s. The key aircraft manufacturers – Ernst Heinkel, Willy Messerschmitt and Hugo Junkers – all had experience of developing high performance civil aircraft before 1933.

After 1935 the air force expanded rapidly. By 1939 there were around 600,000 personnel and a front-line strength, on the outbreak of war, of 3,609 high-quality aircraft. Goering became commander-in-chief of the new air force in 1935 and appointed other airmen he had known from the war years to high office. His deputy was the former Lufthansa director, Erhard Milch, who was the real driving-force behind the development of the force and its organization. The rapid expansion also relied on recruiting people with an army background, including the first chief of air staff Walther Wever and his successor, Albert Kesselring. The army officers brought with them a view of air power quite different from the British experience. The main emphasis in German air strategy was on co-operation between army and air force to give maximum hitting power to any ground assault. Fighters and dive-bombers were expected to attack and destroy the enemy air force

BELOW An aerial panorama of the destruction of the Polish capital Warsaw during the German-Polish war in September 1939. The Polish authorities were determined to defend the city and the German air force was used to bring about a speedy surrender.

GENERAL HANS JESCHONNEK (1899–1943)

Hans Jeschonnek was appointed Chief of the German Air Force Staff by Hermann Goering on 1 February 1939 after a meteoric rise through the ranks of the fledgling German air force.

He joined the German army aged 15 at the outbreak of the First World War and rose by 1917 to be a lieutenant, at which point he enrolled in the air service. He subsequently returned to army duties and joined the revived air force in September 1933 when it was still secret. He became operations chief in February 1938 and a year later chief of staff. He favoured tactical air power in support of the army, but argued in September 1940 for terror attacks against British cities to achieve a quick end to the war following failure in the Battle of Britain. Struggling later in the war to keep the Allied bombers at bay and subject to growing criticism, he committed suicide at Hitler's headquarters on 18 August 1943.

ABOVE A long line of Messerschmitt Me 109 fighter aircraft under construction in a factory in 1943. The fighter was the mainstay of the German fighter force but was produced in quantities too small for what was needed in 1940. Mass production and rationalization only began to make an impact on German aircraft output later in the war.

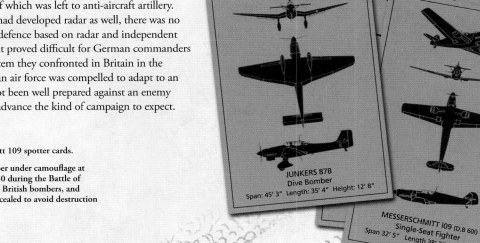

RIGHT German twin-engined "destroyer" aircraft, Messerschmitt Me 110s, flying over Paris on 15 June 1940, two days before the French sought surrender. Paris was earlier declared an open city to avoid German air attacks, but Hitler had already been reluctant to order raids on Paris because of its architectural beauty.

while bombers attacked the enemy frontline and areas of supply. There was no plan for long-range independent bombing attacks, which were regarded as costly and of dubious strategic advantage. A long-range bomber, the Heinkel He 177, was under development in 1939, but it was not expected to be available in numbers until 1942–43.

The air force was organized into four air fleets, each one made up of a component of fighters, dive-bombers, bombers and reconnaissance aircraft. Within each air fleet there would be one or two air divisions, also composed of a mix of aircraft types. The object was to ensure that an air fleet could be assigned to particular army group areas to provide overall air support. The system worked very effectively in the campaign in Poland in 1939 and France in 1940, but it was not designed to undertake an independent air campaign as would be required in the Battle of Britain. The medium bombers carried small bomb loads and had limited range; the fighters were only able to penetrate into a limited area of southern England, even from the bases captured in France and the Low Countries.

Little provision was made in the new German air force for the air defence of Germany, much of which was left to anti-aircraft artillery. Although German scientists had developed radar as well, there was no comprehensive system of air defence based on radar and independent fighter units. For this reason it proved difficult for German commanders to grasp the nature of the system they confronted in Britain in the summer of 1940. The German air force was compelled to adapt to an operation for which it had not been well prepared against an enemy who had anticipated well in advance the kind of campaign to expect.

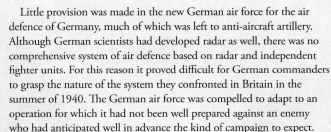

RIGHT Junkers 87B and Messerschmitt 109 spotter cards.

BELOW RIGHT A Heinkel He 111 bomber under camouflage at Marquise near Calais in August 1940 during the Battle of Britain. German bases were close to British bombers, and aircraft had to be dispersed and concealed to avoid destruction on the ground.

JUNKERS 87B
Dive Bomber
Span: 45' 3" Length: 35' 4" Height: 12' 8"

MESSERSCHMITT 109 (D.B 60I)
Single-Seat Fighter
Span 32' 5" Length 28' 3" Height 8' 4"

WILLY MESSERSCHMITT (1898–1978)

Messerschmitt was the most famous German aircraft designer of his generation, responsible for the standard German air force fighter, the Me 109, and the development of the first successful jet aircraft, the Me 262. The son of a wine merchant, Messerschmitt showed an early fascination with the novelty of aircraft design. In 1917, he served briefly in the German army, before studying engineering in Munich. It was during his studies that he founded the Messerschmitt Aircraft Construction Company in Bamberg. Later on, he also worked closely with the Bavarian Aircraft Works (founded in 1927), and the two companies eventually merged. This explains the prefix Bf (Bayerische Flugzeugwerke) originally attached to the 109 series fighter. He joined the National Socialist Party in 1933 and supported the regime's policies, including the use of concentration camp labour to build his aircraft during the war. He was prohibited from working on aircraft after his denazification hearing, but in 1955 he was again designing aircraft for the new German air force.

DOWDING VERSUS GOERING

There was a striking contrast between the two commanders who faced each other for the Battle of Britain in the summer of 1940. Hugh Dowding was effectively commander of the defensive battle, although he was also responsible to the chief of the air staff, Air Chief Marshal Sir Cyril Newall and, from October 1940, (acting) Air Chief Marshal Sir Charles Portal. Hermann Goering, promoted to Reich Marshal by Hitler in July 1940 as a reward for the success of the air force in the conquest of France, was the German commander-in-chief for the air campaign against Britain.

Dowding was a man of 58 with a long and distinguished career behind him. As a commander he was older than was usual and had been due to retire in 1939. His replacement suffered an accident and Dowding was kept in post. Twice more in 1940 – once in March and again in July – he was told he must retire, but at Churchill's insistence was kept on as commander until November, when the battle was effectively over. Dowding was born in Scotland, the son of a schoolmaster, joined the army in 1899 and served in India and the Far East. He was a keen sportsman and skier, and learned to fly before the First World War. He joined the Royal Flying Corps in 1914, but

was posted to organize training in 1916. He was retained in the post-war RAF and became director of training in 1926. In 1930, he became responsible for supply and research in the Air Ministry and it was in this capacity that he oversaw the introduction of radar and the development of modern fighter aircraft. In July 1936, he took over as chief of the newly created Fighter Command.

Dowding had a solid reputation as a talented organizer and commander, but his personality was reserved and awkward. He could talk at length about his interests but did not tolerate contradiction or incompetence. He proved to be a single-minded defender of the fighter force against all attempts to divert fighters to functions other than the defence of the United Kingdom. He brought to his command a great deal of technical and tactical experience and understood the many problems faced by pilots in trying to intervene effectively against incoming bombers. His judgement about the possibility of effective defence, and his strenuous efforts to strengthen his force and reorganize its operational practice were vital elements in the outcome of the Battle of Britain.

ABOVE Dowding inspects a passing out parade of aircraft apprentices at the Halton School of Technical Training on 19 December 1933. Dowding was the Air Member for Supply and Research at the time, with a strong interest in the technical development of the force.

BELOW Hermann Goering with air force officers on one of his visits to the French front during the Battle of Britain. To his left is the German fighter commander Adolf Galland.

SIR ARCHIBALD SINCLAIR (1890–1970)

Goering's direct opposite on the British side was the air minister, Archibald Sinclair. But unlike the German system, the air minister was not simultaneously the commander-in-chief of the air force. Sinclair began an army career in the Life Guards, and served in France throughout the First World War. He became Churchill's secretary at the War Office between 1919 and 1921. In 1922, he began a political career as Liberal MP for Caithness and Sutherland, a constituency he represented until 1945. In 1940, he was appointed air minister by Churchill and became an enthusiast for the strategic bombing of Germany, a policy that he defended against all criticism in parliament. He was defeated in the 1945 election, and was created Viscount Thurso in 1952, acting as leader of the Liberal Party in the House of Lords. He retired from public life in 1964.

LEFT Hermann Goering and the head of the air force technical office, Ernst Udet, watch air manoeuvres on the German Pomeranian coast in the late 1930s. Although unschooled in either strategy or aviation technology, Goering took a very active part in shaping the German air force in the 1930s.

RIGHT After the war Goering was captured and put on trial at Nuremberg for a range of war crimes. He sits on the far left, second row in this courtroom photograph taken during the trial.

GENERAL ERNST UDET (1896–1941)

A well known air ace from the First World War, Ernst Udet flew with the famous Richthofen squadron under the command of Hermann Goering. In the 1920s, he became a popular air stuntman and film star until he was recruited by Goering to join the newly formed German air force. He joined the National Socialist Party and in 1936 became head of the air force Technical Office where he advocated dive-bombing as the most effective form of bomb attack. In 1939, he was created General Quartermaster of the Air Force in charge of all procurement and technical development. A bon viveur and womanizer, Udet was completely inadequate to the responsibilities of his job. When it was evident that German aircraft production and development had stagnated thanks to his failures, he committed suicide in November 1941 and was given a state funeral.

BELOW King George VI and Queen Elizabeth visit Dowding at Bentley Priory in September 1940. She later complained that Dowding never stopped talking. He could seem reserved, but on issues which interested him was notoriously voluble.

Hermann Goering was, like Dowding, a young army officer before 1914 who became fascinated by flying. He was posted to the new German air force and on the death of von Richthofen, the famous "red baron", he became commander of the squadron. After the war, he became a commercial traveller who flew occasional air show stunts. In 1922 he met Adolf Hitler and his future was transformed. He commanded the Stormtroopers (SA) in 1923 at the time of Hitler's failed coup in Bavaria and was forced to flee abroad. He returned in 1927 and threw himself into politics. He became one of the first National Socialist parliamentary deputies and by 1932 was president of the German parliament. In 1933, he entered the Hitler cabinet and remained a minister until 1945. In 1935, he was appointed commander-in-chief of the German air force, a post he held until almost the end of the war, when Hitler stripped him of office in the belief that Goering was trying to supplant him.

Unlike Dowding, Goering had no administrative or command experience. He was a gaudy, ambitious and ruthless individual who used his many offices to create a sumptuous, almost regal lifestyle. He relied on others to undertake much of the routine work of high office, but was always quick to take the credit for their achievements. He was neither stupid nor entirely indolent, but he lacked the capacity to make serious technical decisions and, despite his jealous guardianship of the air force, was unable to prevent it being used largely in support of Germany's powerful and influential army. He contributed little to the air battles of 1940 except to bully and exhort his subordinates. In 1940, he was given the opportunity to show what the air force could achieve on its own in the Battle of Britain. Its eventual failure to subdue the RAF began the slow erosion of Hitler's confidence in Goering's capacity to deliver what he promised.

HITLER TURNS TO BRITAIN

◎ JULY 1940

The situation facing Adolf Hitler in the summer of 1940 was quite unexpected and left him uncertain as to his next moves. When German forces launched their attack on the Western states on 10 May 1940, there was no certainty that a quick victory would be the result. Yet so effective was the German battle plan, Operation Sickle Cut, that the combined forces of the Netherlands, Belgium, France and Britain were unable to prevent a swift and comprehensive defeat. The Dutch army surrendered on 14 May, and the Belgian army on 28 May. The British Expeditionary Force was forced to retreat back to Britain from Dunkirk, undefeated but without its equipment. On 17 June, France sued for an armistice and the war on Continental Europe ended after just six weeks of fighting.

German leaders thought that with the French defeated, Britain would now sue for peace since there no longer seemed any sense in continuing the war. On 23 June, Hitler's Propaganda Minister, Joseph Goebbels, told his staff, "We are very close to the end of the war." Hitler informed the army chief of staff that he regarded an invasion as "very hazardous", and he expected that political and diplomatic pressure would bring Britain to the conference table. Nevertheless, the German armed forces had already begun to plan for possible action against England. The German navy had been preparing contingency plans for an invasion since November 1939, and in May and June the navy's commander-in-chief, Grand Admiral Erich Raeder, suggested to Hitler the possibility of just such an operation. Later in June, the German army also began preliminary research into an invasion of southern England. Not until 7 July did Hitler order the armed forces to prepare definite plans for the continuation of the war against Britain and only on 16 July did he sign War Directive 16 for "Operation Sealion", the codename for an invasion.

Hitler still counted on Britain seeking a political solution. Various hints from British sources suggested that a peaceful settlement might be possible and on 19 July in a session of the German parliament, Hitler gave a speech designed to open the way for a possible negotiated settlement. He said he had no desire to destroy the British Empire and was prepared to consider terms, albeit "as a conqueror". The British government rejected the proposal formally on 22 July, since Churchill and his cabinet had no reason to trust German good faith. On 23 July, Goebbels told a press conference, "Gentlemen, there will be war!" Plans were set in motion to mount a seaborne invasion of the southern English counties of Kent and Sussex with 13 divisions of 260,000 men. There were strong doubts expressed through July about its feasibility, from Hitler downwards. It was evident that only the elimination of the RAF and the bombing of British military targets would create conditions to give an invasion any chance of success.

ABOVE RIGHT A cavalcade of cars on its way to the German Reich Chancellery during the victory parade for the defeat of France on 6 July 1940. The victory opened the way to German domination of Continental Europe.

BELOW The French destroyer Bourrasque sinking off the French port of Dunkirk laden with troops during the Dunkirk evacuation in late May and early June 1940. The loss of almost all British equipment in France persuaded Hitler that an invasion of England might be possible.

ADOLF HITLER (1889–1945)

Adolf Hitler was born in Braunau am Inn, Austria, the son of a customs official. He had ambitions to become an architect, but lacked sufficient talent. In 1914, he volunteered for service in the German army and became a "runner" between the lines, decorated twice for bravery. In 1919, he joined a small radical nationalist party, the German Workers' Party, and by 1921 had become its leader under the changed title of National Socialist German Workers' Party. He staged a failed coup d'état in 1923 and was briefly imprisoned. He campaigned against the Versailles Treaty and demanded a national revival and German "living space". On becoming ruler of Germany in 1933, he launched large-scale rearmament. By 1938, when he became the armed forces' supreme commander, he had formed plans for German expansion in Eastern Europe. In 1939, he attacked Poland in the belief that Britain and France would back down. During the world war that resulted he tried to conquer most of Europe and Western Asia in order to establish a German empire. He also authorized the mass killing of Europe's Jews. In 1945, with Allied armies closing on Berlin, he committed suicide in his underground bunker.

SS INFORMATION HANDBOOK GB

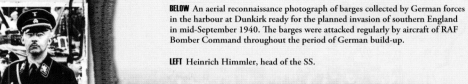

In the summer of 1940, the SS officer Walter Schellenberg, responsible for counter-espionage in Office IVE of the Gestapo organization, helped to draw up a comprehensive guide for the SS and secret policemen who would be trying to make Britain a secure part of Hitler's empire after the success of Operation Sealion. The handbook covered all the main areas of public life, including the masons, the churches and the British intelligence services, on which the writers seemed particularly well informed. Appended to the survey was a list of individuals who might be subject to arrest and imprisonment once the Germans had arrived. An SS colonel Dr Franz Six, later tried for war crimes, was to have been the commander of the Einsatzkommandos (Action Commands) carrying out the arrests. The list included both Neville Chamberlain and Winston Churchill, and the distinguished philosopher Bertrand Russell. Some 20,000 copies of the handbook were made, but were destroyed in Berlin during a bombing raid in 1943.

The preliminary destruction of British air power, and a combined air and naval assault on British shipping and ports were authorized as the first stage of Germany's Battle of Britain.

There has been much speculation about whether Hitler was ever serious about invading Britain. At the same time as Operation Sealion was being prepared, preliminary discussions began between Hitler and his military staff about a possible blow against the Soviet Union. On 31 July, Hitler announced for the first time the possibility of an invasion in the east as a means of removing any prospect Britain might have of continuing the war by relying on Soviet assistance. There is, nonetheless, little doubt that Hitler looked for a possible cheap victory in the West as long as the RAF could be eliminated and Britain, as a result, frightened into submission. "If results of air warfare are unsatisfactory," he also announced on 31 July, "invasion preparations will be stopped." The defeat of the RAF thus became the central aim of German strategy, without which a more ambitious campaign against Britain could not be mounted with any serious chance of success.

ABOVE Native troops man Italian artillery in Egypt on 13 October 1940. Italy's North African army crossed into Egypt in September to put additional pressure on Britain at the height of the invasion scare.

BELOW Hitler addresses the German parliament in the Kroll Opera House in Berlin on 19 July 1940 in order to make a "peace offer" to Britain. Behind Hitler sits Hermann Goering, who was also president of the Reichstag.

BELOW An aerial reconnaissance photograph of barges collected by German forces in the harbour at Dunkirk ready for the planned invasion of southern England in mid-September 1940. The barges were attacked regularly by aircraft of RAF Bomber Command throughout the period of German build-up.

LEFT Heinrich Himmler, head of the SS.

THE BATTLE BEGINS

Even before any decision had been taken to undertake an invasion of Britain, German air and naval forces had already begun operations against British trade and shipping. The German navy's commander-in-chief, Grand Admiral Raeder, favoured a blockade of British trade by sea and air attacks which would cripple Britain's capacity to supply its armed forces and feed the population. The idea of blockading Britain was approved by Hitler and it remained an important element in German strategy throughout the period of the Battle of Britain and the subsequent Blitz. Between June 1940 and the end of the year, more than three million tons of merchant shipping was sunk, of which around 350,000 tons was accounted for by air attack. The quantity of goods imported into Britain fell by one-fifth during the period.

During June and July, the German air force, operating from its new bases spread across northern France and the Low Countries, began a series of probing attacks against targets in southern England to test the defences there and to help in developing effective tactics for attack. Since the German side had not expected to wage a war of this kind, the preparatory attacks were useful in giving pilots experience of what to expect when the full air battle was joined. They attacked in small formations, but the targets selected were so random that British commanders could make little sense of them. One attack on 31 July left bombs scattered from eastern Cornwall to Monmouth, on the Welsh border, most of which fell in open country or on small villages and towns. By the end of July, 258 civilians had been killed but only limited damage done to military facilities. The early attacks also gave Fighter Command the opportunity to refine its operations and discuss tactics. The protective fighter belt was spread further to the west with the creation of 10 Group and additional radar stations were built. Both sides waited for the real battle to begin.

German air commanders only finalized the operational plans for the elimination of the RAF late in July 1940. On 1 August, Hitler issued a directive calling on the German air force "to overpower the English air force … in the shortest possible time". The German side was confident that the RAF could be defeated quickly. The army chief of staff, General Franz Halder, was told that the operation to secure air superiority would take at most between two weeks and a month.

ABOVE Life in an English country pub continues almost as normal following a bombing raid in July 1940. Small hit-and-run raids were carried out all through the summer as the German air force probed the defences and refined their tactics.

RIGHT The German long-range reconnaissance and bomber aircraft Focke-Wulf 200. Known as the "Condor", the aircraft played an important early role in the war against British shipping but was vulnerable to faster-flying fighter aircraft.

GRAND ADMIRAL ERICH RAEDER (1876–1960)

Erich Raeder was commander-in-chief of the German navy at the start of the Second World War, a post he had held since 1928. Born in the port city of Hamburg, Raeder joined the navy in 1894 and rose rapidly through the ranks. He was not an enthusiast for Hitler, but recognized that in the Third Reich he could fulfil his dream of rebuilding a powerful German navy. He realized how weak his force was in 1939 when faced with the British and French fleets, but hoped that a successful sea-air blockade might force Britain out of the war. After a series of naval disasters, he was finally relieved of office in 1943. He was tried at the Nuremberg trials in 1945–46 and sentenced to life imprisonment, but served only nine years before his release.

German air intelligence assumed that the RAF was already weakened by the battle in France and estimated British aircraft production at only half its true figure. The difficulty faced by the German air force was the uncertainty about whether an invasion would actually take place and the wide range of different targets they were ordered to attack. On 2 August, Goering ordered what he called "Eagle Attack" against RAF bases, ports, factories and units of the Royal Navy; the following day the air force chief of staff, Hans Jeschonnek, additionally ordered attacks on radar stations. The actual start of the campaign – known as "Eagle Day" – had to be postponed in early August because of bad weather and the slow recovery from the heavy losses inflicted in the battle of France. In the end, Eagle Day was launched only on 13 August.

The two air forces that faced each other for the battle in August 1940 were more evenly matched than the popular view of the battle suggests. By 9 August, Fighter Command had 1,032 fighter aircraft with a further 424 in reserve for immediate use. The German single-engine fighter force on 10 August numbered 1,011. Fighter Command had on average 1,400 fighter pilots available during the weeks of August, the German fighter force only 1,100–1,200, with 800–900 regularly available for operations. In addition the German Air Fleets 2 and 3 in northern France and the Low Countries, and Air Fleet 5 in Norway, mustered around 250 twin-engined fighters, 280 dive-bombers and 1,000 serviceable bombers. British Bomber Command had around 500 bombers by August. These were the forces that fought out the Battle of Britain when the German onslaught was finally launched.

ABOVE The Welsh port of Swansea at dawn after a third night of bombing in August 1940. German aircraft attacked port cities as part of a broad plan to blockade Britain into surrender and to disrupt the British war economy.

TOP RIGHT An RAF sergeant plotting a course at an RAF Coastal Command base in January 1940.

COASTAL COMMAND

Coastal Command was created in the reorganization of 1936. Its role was to provide a dedicated air force for attacks on enemy shipping in the seas around Britain, for protection of British convoys, and for reconnaissance over sea and coastal areas. On the outbreak of war, it was commanded by Air Chief Marshal Frederick Bowhill with three Group headquarters at Plymouth, Chatham and Rosyth, where the airmen worked side-by-side with naval staff. Coastal Command had 19 squadrons of largely obsolescent aircraft on the outbreak of war but expanded rapidly as the war at sea became a greater threat in 1940. From May 1940 onwards, Coastal Command had to undertake dangerous long-range reconnaissance missions over the North Sea and the Channel, and losses of its slow and vulnerable aircraft were high. Over a sixth-month period, the command lost 158 aircraft and 600 crew out of an August 1940 strength of only 470 planes. In the war at sea, the command could contribute little with old-fashioned or ineffective equipment. It became a more modern and effective fighting force only from 1941 onwards.

BELOW The wreckage of Stanley Street in the south coast city of Portsmouth after a heavy raid in August 1940. Portsmouth was one of a handful of ports hit heavily over the summer months, and long before the onset of the Blitz on London and other cities.

THE HURRICANE AND THE SPITFIRE

BOTTOM Reginald Mitchell (far right), designer of the Spitfire, at work on an S6B seaplane which won the Schneider Trophy in 1928 at a speed of 528 kph (328 mph).

Two aircraft, the Hawker Hurricane and Supermarine Spitfire, were the mainstays of Fighter Command during the Battle of Britain. They were both developed in the mid-1930s during the period when the RAF was searching for a high-performance modern monoplane fighter. Both depended on the simultaneous development of the Rolls-Royce Merlin engine, without which the high performance of the two fighters would not have been possible.

RIGHT The Supermarine Spitfire Mark 1A flying over cloud. The legendary fighter was introduced slowly during 1939 and early 1940, but by the time of the battle made up around 35 per cent of Fighter Command's numbers.

BELOW A flight of six Hawker Hurricane Mark IIB fighters from 601 Squadron RAF stationed at Duxford in Cambridgeshire. They are seen here flying over Thaxted in Essex.

The Hurricane and Spitfire were very different aircraft but were created at almost exactly the same time. The Hurricane was designed in 1934–35 by the Hawker Aircraft Company's Sydney Camm in response to an Air Ministry specification. His first design was turned down, but he immediately began a "private venture" design built around the Merlin engine which the RAF liked and ordered into production in June 1936. The design was based on the techniques used in Hawker's successful biplane fighters, and the thick wing, covered with fabric rather than metal, and two-blade propeller made the aircraft obsolescent by the standards of the new generation of fighters being produced in Europe. It was nevertheless a very sturdy aircraft, with a tight turning circle. It was easy to fly and easily repaired. By December 1938, it was in service with the RAF and 500 had been delivered by the outbreak of war.

The Spitfire – named by the owner of the Vickers Supermarine Aircraft Company after his daughter, a little "spitfire" – began life as Type 300, an advanced fighter design by the chief designer at Supermarine, R. J. Mitchell. It, too, was planned around the evolving Rolls-Royce PV-XII engine, soon to be christened the Merlin. Mitchell adopted a number of new advances, many drawn from the United States aviation industry, including a retractable undercarriage, light thin wings with a characteristic elliptical shape, and a closed cockpit. It was modern monoplane design with an all-metal fuselage, light, easy to handle and capable of regular modification and upgrading. It had a top speed during the Battle of Britain of at least 560 kph (350 mph) compared with around 530 kph (330 mph) for the Hurricane.

REGINALD MITCHELL (1895–1937)

R. J. Mitchell began his engineering career helping to design high-performance locomotives. He learned aeronautics in his spare time, and became an aeronautical engineer for the Vickers Supermarine works in Southampton, where he was appointed chief designer in 1919. He designed some 24 aircraft, but is best known as the designer of the Spitfire, which he began working on in summer 1934. He based its high performance on his designs for the Schneider Trophy-winning S6B racing aircraft and another fighter project, the Type 224, which the RAF rejected. He was a shy but single-minded personality, who struggled against ill health in the last years of his life while completing the Spitfire. He died of cancer in June 1937, and his design was taken over and improved by his successor, Joseph Smith.

BELOW The Merlin engine under construction. Here the crank case assembly bay can be seen, with cylinder studs in the process of being fitted.

THE ROLLS-ROYCE MERLIN ENGINE

The Rolls-Royce Merlin engine, named after the small bird of prey, was one of the war's most successful aero-engines. Around 150,000 were produced, used principally in the British Spitfire, Hurricane, Lancaster, Halifax and Mosquito, and later in the American P-51 Mustang fighter. A liquid-cooled V12 piston engine, the Merlin, first designated the PV-12, was developed in 1934–35. It suffered a great many teething problems until the war, by which time Rolls-Royce had produced an engine of high reliability, capable of regular modification and upgrading. When used with high-octane fuels, the engine gave British fighters a great boost during the Battle of Britain, though it could not be used easily in a steep dive until the invention in March 1941 of "Miss Shilling's orifice", a diaphragm developed by the engineer Beatrice Shilling to prevent fuel from escaping from the carburettor during a dive.

The Air Ministry ordered Mitchell to produce a prototype in January 1935 and the first Spitfire flew on 5 March 1936, four months after the first Hurricane. It proved so successful that in June 1936 the Ministry ordered over 300 aircraft, but production hold-ups led to the proposed cancellation of the model in 1938. Vickers succeeded in persuading the RAF to persevere with it and within three years the Spitfire became the backbone of the British wartime fighter force. The first Spitfires entered service on 4 August 1938 with 19 Squadron stationed at Duxford, near Cambridge. The last Spitfire flight with the RAF took place in 1957.

Spitfire production took some time to get going during 1939 and 1940, and during the Battle of Britain there were more Hurricane than Spitfire squadrons. The Spitfire also took higher losses, partly because they were detailed to attack the German Me109 fighters while the Hurricanes mainly engaged the slower-flying bombers. At the end of the battle there were still 33 Hurricane squadrons against 20 Spitfire squadrons. The Hurricanes had some disadvantages in combat but the decision to replace the two-blade propeller with the standard Rotol constant-speed propeller, which became standard during the battle, improved performance a good deal. So too did the decision to replace fabric wings with metal-covered wings. The biggest disadvantage was the position of the fuel tank in front of the pilot, which resulted in severe burns for pilots when their tanks were hit by enemy fire. The Merlin-powered Spitfire was a successful design except for the inability to dive sharply without losing fuel supply to the engine or placing undue stress on the pilot.

In all, some 14,000 Hurricanes were built during its combat lifespan, including modified designs such as the Sea Hurricane, which operated from aircraft carriers. There were 20,351 Spitfires built, the most of any wartime Allied fighter, and there were 24 variants. There was also a version for use at sea, the Seafire. Over the years it is the Spitfire that has become the iconic aircraft of the Battle of Britain, but the sturdy workhorse Hurricane also contributed a great deal to the success of the RAF in 1940.

BELOW The Spitfire production line at the Vickers Supermarine factory in Southampton c.1939–40. Production was decentralized to avoid the risk of bomb damage and a large factory set up by the Morris car manufacturer, Lord Nuffield, at Castle Bromwich.

DETECTING THE ENEMY

In 1934, the Air Ministry established a scientific committee to investigate the whole question of effective air defence. It was chaired by Henry Tizard and included the Air Ministry's own Director of Scientific Research, H. E. Wimperis. At its first meeting it was decided to ask the superintendent of the Radio Department at the National Physical Laboratory, Robert Watson-Watt, to supply advice on the possibility of using radio waves either to disable aircraft or to detect them in flight. Watson-Watt rejected the first, but suggested that radio pulses could be reflected from aircraft and the results recorded, so allowing enemy aircraft to be tracked. On 26 February 1935, a first experiment was carried out at Weedon in Northamptonshire which clearly demonstrated that an aircraft reflected electro-magnetic energy and that those reflections could be detected by the use of a cathode-ray apparatus. This experiment launched the British development of what became known as RDF or radio direction finding, and later still came to be called radar.

Radar research was not confined to Britain. In the mid-1930s research and development work was also carried out in Germany, Japan, France, Italy, the United States, The Netherlands and the Soviet Union, though the most significant use of radar was to be found by the outbreak of war only in Britain and Germany. The first British radar sets for detecting aircraft were operational by the end of 1939. The possibilities of radar were regarded in Britain as so important that plans were laid down as early as the autumn of 1935 for a protective string of radar stations around the British coast. The system became known as Home Chain and final approval for a network of 20 stations using so-called "Home Chain" radar was granted in August 1937. By this time Watson-Watt and his team had developed effective transmitting and detecting equipment. When war came in September 1939, there were 18 Home Chain stations operational around the English coast and two in Scotland.

The importance of radar lay in the system designed to transmit the information seen on the radar screen quickly to the operations rooms of Fighter Command. The information was first sent to a "filter room", then on to the Command's chief operations room at Bentley Priory and from there to the fighter sectors involved. Radar could generally detect incoming aircraft at around 130 kilometres (80 miles) distance and the development of an Identification Friend or Foe (IFF) system meant that it was possible to distinguish enemy from friendly aircraft. A number of Home Chain Low stations were also developed to cope with aircraft flying at lower than 300 metres (1,000 feet), but could

LEFT A group of airmen and WAAF operators at work in the receiver hut at the radar station at Ventnor on the Isle of Wight during the battle. The information from radar detection could be sent immediately by telephone to Fighter Command headquarters.

ROBERT WATSON-WATT (1892–1973)

Robert Watson-Watt, a descendant of James Watt, the inventor of the steam engine, was a radio engineer who began his career with the Meteorological Office in 1915. Here he began work on predicting thunderstorms by the use of radio signals. He was assigned to the Air Ministry and in 1927 was made director of the Radio Research Station in the National Physical Laboratory. His work attracted the attention of the Air Ministry in the 1930s and he led the team that pioneered the first true radio detection of aircraft in 1935. In 1938, he became Director of Communications Development in the Royal Aircraft Establishment and a year later was appointed Scientific Adviser (Telecommunications) for the Air Ministry. After the war he became an engineering consultant in Canada and the United States. In 1966 he married Dame Katherine Trefusis-Forbes, the woman who had been the first commander of the Women's Auxiliary Air Force.

BELOW A photograph of the White Cliffs of Dover taken from a German aircraft during the Battle of Britain. The radar chain towers are clearly visible and in the background smoke can be seen from a bombing raid on Canterbury. The German air forces failed to attack the radar stations heavily or consistently.

detect aircraft at a distance of only 50 kilometres (30 miles). Radar did not yet work effectively inland, so that Fighter Command was forced to rely on ground observation of aircraft once they had crossed the coast. This was the job of the 30,000 members of the Observer Corps whose posts were supplied with grid maps, a height estimator and a telephone linked directly to the Fighter Command communications network. Although ground observation could supply estimates of height that were widely inaccurate, the general direction of attack could be observed and aircraft scrambled to intercept.

Radar was an important element of the air defence system but it was not entirely reliable. It was possible for height estimations to be wrong, and the time between a sighting and the order to scramble could take a minimum of four minutes while the detected aircraft could be across the English Channel in only six minutes. Improvements in radar technology, important though they were, left some radar stations temporarily inoperable while the new equipment was being installed. Nonetheless, the system worked well enough to permit a reasonable knowledge of the enemy's intentions. The German side never guessed the extent to which radar was integrated into the whole fighter control system and failed to press home attacks on radar stations when these were ordered in mid-August 1940. As a result, the Home Chain continued to supply radar intelligence throughout the battle.

LEFT The cover of a popular book on aircraft recognition. Books were sold in thousands so that ordinary people could tell friend from foe, but it was easy even for skilled pilots to mistake their own aircraft for the enemy.

BELOW Observer Corps armband.

ABOVE An Observer Corps crew in an observation post during the Battle of Britain. The 30,000 observers were a vital link in the web of detection and communication.

SIR HENRY TIZARD (1885–1959)

Henry Tizard wanted a career in the Royal Navy but was prevented by poor eyesight from joining. After studying chemistry and mathematics at Oxford, he began a study of aeronautics. During the First World War he became an officer in the Royal Flying Corps responsible for experimental equipment and ended the war in 1919 as an officer in the RAF. He returned to Oxford but then took a post in the government Department of Scientific and Industrial Research. In 1929, he became rector of Imperial College, London, a post he held until 1942. In 1933, he was appointed chair of the Air Ministry's Aeronautical Research Committee where he played a key role in the development of the British radar defences. Between 1948 and 1952, he was chief scientific adviser to the Ministry of Defence, where he pioneered the serious scientific study of UFOs.

The official start of the campaign to destroy the RAF, codenamed Adlerangriff (Eagle Attack) was supposed to start on 5 August, following Hitler's directive of the first day of that month. The German air force staff decided to wait until 10 August, but poor weather reports brought postponement for a further day. The decision was finally taken to begin the campaign, despite unreliable weather, on 13 August. This was to be Adlertag, Eagle Day.

Following operations against the radar network the previous day, the first wave of attacks began early in the morning. Some 200 German bombers and fighters of Air Fleets 2 and 3 approached on a broad front from bases around Amiens, Dieppe and Cherbourg. They were met in the first instance by 120 fighters, already alerted by radar to the approaching threat. The bombers failed to attack any Fighter Command station, while the inability to supply an effective fighter escort exposed many of them to repeated attacks by British fighters. A further operation around midday was undertaken by Me 110 twin-engined fighters, which arrived over England without the bombers they were supposed to be escorting, flying in a circle to provide each

plane with fire cover. The pilots nicknamed the tactic "the circle of death" because of the high losses that resulted. The force was mauled by squadrons of 10 Group scrambled from Warmwell and Exeter, and a squadron of 11 Group from Tangmere. Five German planes were shot down before they retreated back to France.

In the afternoon, a second major wave, made up of around 120 aircraft, was sent from Air Fleet 2 against targets in Kent and Air Fleet 3 against the air base at Middle Wallop and other targets in the Southampton area. Warned well in advance, there were squadrons from 10 and 11 Group waiting for the new incursions. The attack on the Southampton area was met by a vigorous counter-attack, but this time the bombers were escorted by a large element of Me 109s

TOP RIGHT Barrage balloons on the skyline over London. London was defended by a mixture of balloons, anti-aircraft guns and a network of fighter stations on the fringes of the capital.

RIGHT A German squadron commander receiving the reports of his squadron crews after returning from a mission over southern England on 13 August 1940. German aircraft flew a total of 1,485 sorties that day and lost 47 aircraft.

BELOW A group of German officers look across the English Channel at the White Cliffs of Dover. Like Napoleon, this was as far as the German armed forces were to get.

FIELD MARSHAL WOLFRAM VON RICHTHOFEN (1895-1945)

A cousin of the famous "Red Baron", Manfred von Richthofen, Wolfram was commissioned in a German hussar regiment in 1913 before training to fly in 1917. In 1918, he became a pilot in his cousin's squadron. After the war he trained as an engineer and returned to the army in 1923, where he worked in the secret preparation of a new German air force. In 1933 he became chief of the Development Division in the newly formed German Air Ministry, and was promoted in 1936 to lieutenant colonel. He led the Condor Legion sent by Hitler to aid Franco in the Spanish Civil War and was responsible for ordering the notorious air attack on Guernica in April 1937. He also led the German air force unit that attacked Poland first, early on the morning of 1 September. In the Battle of Britain he was commander of the VIII Fliegerkorps, which he continued to lead in the Balkan campaign in 1941 and in the assault on the Soviet Union. He was promoted to field marshal in 1943, but the following year was diagnosed with a brain tumour. He retired from service and died in an American POW camp on 12 July 1945.

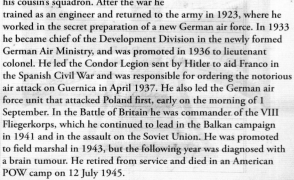

KAMPFGRUPPE 100

On 18 November 1939, two squadrons of German bombers were activated as "pathfinder" units tasked with leading bombers accurately to distant targets. On 13 July 1940, a third squadron was activated. The force was named Kampfgruppe 100 (Bomber Group 100) and received special training in navigating with a new system of radio beams known as X-Gerät. Using four radio beams from different directions, the force was able to arrive over the target with a high level of accuracy. During the Battle of Britain, the unit was commanded by Captain Kurt Aschenbrenner. On the night of 13 August, the group first attacked the large Spitfire factory at Castle Bromwich in Birmingham with 11 bombs, doing little serious damage. Later Kampfgruppe 100 led the major raids against British cities during the Blitz.

and fierce dogfights broke out. The bombers failed to find the Middle Wallop station and scattered their bombs widely over the southern counties in their path. The aircraft from Air Fleet 2 took advantage of cloud cover over Kent, but the bombers only succeeded in attacking a Coastal Command base while others dropped their bombs blind. Over the whole of Eagle Day, no damage was done to Fighter Command stations or to radar installations.

The balance of losses on the first official day of the campaign strongly favoured the defence. The German air force lost a total of 47 aircraft, while Fighter Command lost only 13, with seven of the pilots saved. The greatest failure exposed that day was the Ju 87 dive-bomber, which was too slow in combat with British fighters. Over the first few days of Eagle Attack some dive-bomber units had 50 per cent losses. On 18 August, they were withdrawn from combat. In the days following Eagle Day, except for 15 August, the weather prevented heavy attacks, but the air fleets continued to probe the British defences. Air Fleet 3 sent over small numbers of unescorted bombers aimed at particular targets, but they faced heavy opposition and found it difficult to locate targets. On 15 August, it was possible to send over a heavy force again and the fighting that day was fiercer than it had been on Eagle Day. That day bombers were also sent against targets in northern England from bases in Norway, with disastrous results. The German forces lost 75 aircraft, Fighter Command some 34. A repeat of heavy raids on 18 August produced the fiercest fighting of the battle, with 100 German aircraft destroyed or damaged for the loss of 74 British fighters.

Eagle Day was a disappointment to the German commanders. Both air fleets failed to identify a clear pattern of targets and difficulties encountered in the battle meant that even those targets selected were either subjected to minor damage or not hit at all. Over the following days an effort was made to co-ordinate attacks more effectively and to identify targets that might really undermine the capacity of Fighter Command to maintain its concerted and deadly resistance.

LEFT The American journalist Edward R. Murrow at work in London during the battle and the Blitz. The young 32-year old Murrow became a household name in America with his reports of the fighting for CBS Radio. His broadcasts all began with the phrase, "This is London". He stayed throughout the bombing that followed the air battle and returned to the United States in late 1941, shortly before the attack on Pearl Harbor.

BELOW LEFT A German air force reconnaissance photograph of the airbase at Coltishall in Norfolk in 1940. Careful aerial reconnaissance enabled German aircraft to pinpoint their attacks on individual air stations.

BELOW A Messerschmitt Me 110 spotter card.

BOTTOM A German Heinkel He 111P medium-bomber shot down at Charterhouse in Somerset by 92 Squadron on 14 August, the day following Eagle Day. The bombers were no match for the new generation of fast interceptor fighters.

MESSERSCHMITT Me. 110 (2-D, B, 601)
Twin-Engine Fighter
Span: 53' 3" Length: 40' 0" Height: 10' 9"

THE ASSAULT ON FIGHTER COMMAND
◎ AUGUST 1940

The assault on Fighter Command which began with "Eagle Day" was supposed to result in the elimination of the RAF's capacity to contest the skies over southern England in four days of intensive operations. The attacks on RAF airfields, radar stations and communications began on 12 August and went on with differing levels of intensity until early September, long after the four days originally assigned to the campaign.

Between 12 August and 6 September, there were 53 main attacks against RAF airfields, though only 32 targeted fighter stations. There were also a great many smaller attacks which were designed to keep up the pressure on the RAF's organization, which the German air force later calculated at a figure of 1,000 raids. All but two of the attacks against fighter bases were made against Park's 11 Group in south-east England. The scale of the attacks was at times limited by the weather, but also by the degree of resistance shown by Fighter Command in the endless dogfights that developed between the two sides over the three weeks of the campaign.

The assault began on 12 August with six major raids against radar stations. These achieved very little, partly because Fighter Command had organized subsidiary facilities in case a Home Chain station was temporarily out of operation. After this, raids against radar stations

were few in number, since the German side assumed that they were difficult targets to destroy and, moreover, understood little of the integrated nature of the Fighter Command early warning system. From 13 August, the fighter stations and subsidiary airfields became the main battleground. Low-flying German aircraft attempted to destroy British aircraft on the ground, as they had done in Poland and France, but although 56 were destroyed in total, this occurred mainly at the start of the battle. Fighter bases were ordered to disperse and camouflage all aircraft, and a network of subsidiary airfields made it possible to avoid easy detection and to continue flying if a major air station was briefly made inoperable.

By 20 August, it was evident that the order to eliminate the RAF in four days had failed. German attacks began to move further inland against more distant RAF targets, while Goering ordered the final destruction of the RAF with "ceaseless attacks" by day and night against military and industrial targets. Every few days, German air intelligence assured Goering that the battle was almost won. At the

AIR VICE-MARSHAL QUINTIN BRAND (1893-1968)

Quintin Brand, the son of a South African policeman, moved to Britain in 1915 to join the Royal Flying Corps. After serving on the Western Front, he commanded one of the first night-fighter squadrons in Britain in 1918. He remained in the RAF and was knighted in 1920 for an attempted record flight from London to Cape Town. He worked at the Royal Aircraft Establishment in the 1920s, and was Director-General of Aviation in Egypt from 1932 to 1936. He became commander of 10 Group, Fighter Command, when it was activated in 1940 and played an important part in the defence of southern England in 1940. He retired from the RAF in 1943 and moved to Southern Rhodesia (Zimbabwe) in 1952.

ABOVE When the approach of enemy planes was reported, RAF squadrons were "scrambled" to intercept them. Here pilots run towards their waiting Hurricanes.

RIGHT German Junkers Ju 87B dive-bombers flying over the English coast during the Battle of Britain. The dive-bombers were used to attack convoys and shipping as well as RAF installations but they took such high casualties that they were withdrawn from the battle.

GERMAN AIR INTELLIGENCE

One of the great failures in the Battle of Britain was the German air intelligence organization. It was led during the Battle of Britain by Colonel Josef "Beppo" Schmid. The reports produced by his staff about the strength, deployment and operation of Fighter Command, and about the levels of British aircraft production played an important part in encouraging wildly exaggerated expectations about the defeat of the RAF. On 7 August, Air Intelligence reported that the radar stations would tie British squadrons closely to their local airfields and prevent any concentration of effort. Schmid failed to grasp the nature of the link between radar, observation and operations and so underestimated the capacity of Fighter Command to intercept German attacks. Thanks to a stream of poor intelligence provided by German secret agent "Ostro", British aircraft production was estimated at only half its true volume. In early September, Schmid relayed to Goering the news that Fighter Command had been reduced at one point to only 100 serviceable aircraft when the true figure was six times as great.

ABOVE German air intelligence officers scrutinize images taken during the Battle of Britain.

RIGHT A view looking down on the filter room at Fighter Command headquarters where the information was collected from radar and observers, and then fed back to the frontline squadrons.

BACKGROUND A sketch of the aerial battle over an airfield in south-east England drawn by Fred Goodwin, a member of RAF ground crew in summer 1940. He kept a record in pictures of his experience during the war.

end of the month he was told that Fighter Command had lost 791 aircraft against a German loss of only 169. In reality, the losses were more or less even: 444 RAF fighters between 6 August and 2 September; 443 German fighters between 8 and 31 August. Total German losses for that period amounted to a little under 900 aircraft of all types. By the end of August, the cumulative strain on both air forces from three weeks of continuous attritional warfare was profound.

The success of Fighter Command in withstanding the assault on its organization was due to a number of factors. Much of the German effort was devoted to air bases near the Kent and Sussex coasts, particularly Lympne, Manston and Hawkinge, each of which was out of commission for only a few days during the battle. These were regarded by Park and Dowding as emergency fields, while vulnerable aircraft could be pulled back to airfields further inland. Because of the early warning system, the withdrawal of aircraft made little difference to the ability to intercept bombers. Park could also call on the more distant fighter squadrons of 12

and 10 Groups to support his own activities, and on a supply of pilots from other parts of the country who replaced tired and battered squadrons at key points in the contest. Park ordered standing patrols at low level to prevent a surprise bombing attack while Hurricanes were ordered to concentrate on destroying the bombers, since they were responsible for the damage on the ground. Meanwhile, the higher performance Spitfires engaged enemy fighters.

The German force reacted to these tactical changes by withdrawing the vulnerable Ju 87 dive-bombers and the Me 110 twin-engined fighters, both of which had suffered high casualties, and by trying to lure Fighter Command aircraft into unequal battles further out over the English Channel. But there was little that the German side could do to undermine the British communications system, while the high toll on both fighters and bombers led to a sharp decline in the number of serviceable aircraft and to a shortage of skilled pilots. By early September, despite the exaggerated estimates of British losses made on the German side, it was evident that the Eagle Day campaign had failed to achieve its objectives.

The Luftwaffe got a real pasting, nine Junkers being part of Formation of 17 being to ribbons by "Hurry's" being flamed back Sept 27th

The days bag — 133
34
17 pilots

WOMEN IN THE BATTLE OF BRITAIN

Women played an important though often neglected part in the Battle of Britain, not only as volunteer members of the Women's Auxiliary Air Force (created in 1939), but also as members of the Women's Voluntary Service formed in 1938 to offer welfare help during future bombing raids. Women were also well represented in the workforce of the rapidly expanding armaments and aviation industries. They were not allowed to fly in combat, but they ran all the risks that servicemen did if they were based at airfields or in operations rooms. During the bombing, women helpers were exposed to the same dangers faced by the male civil defence personnel.

There had briefly been a Women's Royal Air Force in 1918–20. On 28 June 1939, a new service was created out of 47 RAF companies in the Auxiliary Territorial Service (formed in 1938). It was called the Women's Auxiliary Air Force and its members became usually known by the acronym "WAAFs". In September 1939, there were 1,700 members, but by 1943, after conscription had been introduced, there were 175,000. A table of ranks was introduced in December 1939 equivalent to male ranks, but women were paid only two-thirds of the amount paid to men.

RIGHT Fighter Command Operations Room in which the WAAFs had a key role to play in collecting and collating information and making sure the plot maps were kept entirely up to date.

The Auxiliary Air Force performed a wide variety of support roles for the RAF. They acted as drivers, clerks, telephonists and a host of other service jobs. Their most famous role was during the Battle of Britain when WAAFs could be found at radar stations and in operations rooms helping to plot attacking aircraft and direct the fighters to intercept them. But they also had an important role in interpreting aerial reconnaissance photographs and in other areas of air intelligence. There was also a separate RAF Nursing Service, though female doctors were

BELOW A famous image from the early years of war shows an RAF pilot and a WAAF standing side-by-side. The first women's air force had existed at the end of the First World War but was closed down. The WAAF was founded again in June 1939.

SERVE IN THE WAAF
WITH THE MEN WHO FLY

DAME KATHERINE TREFUSIS-FORBES (1899–1971)

The first commander of the Women's Auxiliary Air Force in the Second World War was Katherine Trefusis-Forbes, a redoubtable woman who ran a kennel business until she volunteered for emergency service work in 1935. She had been a member of the Women's Volunteer Reserve during the First World War and achieved the rank of second lieutenant. In 1939, she played a key part in organizing the support role of women in the RAF, rising to the rank of air chief commandant by October 1943, when she was succeeded by Mary Welsh. She promoted women's services abroad from 1943 and returned to civilian life in 1945. In 1966, she married Robert Watson-Watt, the pioneer of British radar.

integrated into the ranks of the RAF medical services. Later in the war, German women performed many of the same duties as auxiliaries in the German air force.

In June 1938, a second all-female organization was established to cope with the expected threat of air attack. The Women's Voluntary Service for Air Raid Precaution was founded in June 1938 under the auspices of Lady Reading, a volunteer nurse in the First World War and widow of a former Viceroy of India. Its members, recruited countrywide, had a distinctive uniform of green tweed jackets and matching hats. In January 1939, the name was changed to Women's Voluntary Service for Civil Defence to reflect the wide range of roles that women were expected to undertake in a bombing war. The motto of the service was, "The WVS never says no!" The members' functions were chiefly concerned with post-raid welfare, though an important part of their work early in the war was to help administer the vast evacuation of mothers and children from the threatened cities and to place evacuees with families in the reception areas.

With the onset of heavy bombing, the WVS helped to collect clothes and equipment to help bombed-out families and to provide temporary accommodation for those whose homes had been destroyed. They also manned rest centres in or near air raid shelters, and organized mobile canteens to provide hot food for men posted to distant air

stations and observation points. Women were to be found providing direct support to the main civil defence branches: air raid precaution (ARP), the fire service, the ambulance service and public transport.

Not all women accepted that war was necessary or that bombing could not be resisted by different means. The pacifist writer Vera Brittain, who had also been a nurse during the First World War, became a spokesman in 1937 for the pacifist Peace Pledge Union and during 1940 could be found at demonstrations against war in general and against bombing as an instrument of war in particular. Her "Letters to Peace Lovers" were published every fortnight during 1940, distributed to pacifists all over the country. In 1941, during the Blitz, she helped to found a Bombing Restrictions Committee which campaigned for the RAF not to retaliate in kind for German attacks. Though always a small minority, women pacifists helped to give voice to many of the anxieties felt by other women as they came to terms with the demands of total war.

BELOW LEFT Members of the WAAF pack parachutes to be used by pilots when they have to bail out of their aircraft mid-flight.

BOTTOM LEFT A young girl is rescued from a bombed building by a female ARP warden during the bombing of London in 1940. Women civil defence workers played a large part in the rescue and rehabilitation of bomb victims.

WAR WORK FOR WOMEN

During the early stages of the war, women workers were recruited to fill the jobs vacated by men as a result of conscription. Even before the war, around a quarter of the British workforce was female, but it proved necessary to move many of them from inessential industries to work with armaments. The proportion of women workers in the motor and aircraft industries rose from nine per cent in 1939 to 23 per cent two years later, and eventually to over 36 per cent in 1943–44. Women were generally paid at a much lower rate than men, and their work often classified as unskilled even when they performed similar functions to men. In 1940, new wage rates were negotiated but they were still well below male levels, and led to considerable complaint among the growing army of women employed in armaments, who were essential for keeping British war production going.

ABOVE Female workers in a Supermarine Spitfire factory in April 1941.

BELOW The commander of the women's section of the Air Transport Auxiliary (ATA), Pauline Gower, with a group of female pilots and staff from No. 5 Ferry Pilots Pool based at Hatfield, Berkshire. Women began ferrying aircraft in 1939 and eventually 166 served with the ATA, 15 of them losing their lives.

BIGGIN HILL

◎ AUGUST 1940

Biggin Hill in Kent was perhaps the most famous of all the RAF fighter bases during the Battle of Britain. By the end of November, when two Spitfires shot down an Me 109 over the Channel, the station claimed 600 enemy aircraft destroyed. The aces who flew from Biggin Hill included Max Aitken (son of Lord Beaverbrook and a member of the "Millionaires' Squadron"), "Sailor" Malan and John Mungo-Park. The most remarkable thing about Biggin Hill was the fact that it continued to act as a fighter station even when almost all its buildings had been destroyed in air attacks in late August 1940.

The airfield had begun life in January 1917 during the First World War when the Royal Flying Corps established a Wireless Testing Park there. During the interwar years it remained a site for testing RAF equipment, with an emphasis on radio communication. At the start of the war in September 1939, the station was home to two Hurricane squadrons, including 32 Squadron, which had been based there since 1932, and a squadron of twin-engined Blenheims. With the onset of

the Battle of Britain, Biggin Hill found itself in the frontline of 11 Group airfields, a natural target for the German air force in the "Eagle Attack" of August 1940. During the course of the battle the station was home to a total of six squadrons, though the system of rotating squadrons to safer airfields for rest meant that there were seldom more than two squadrons operational at any one time.

The fighters from Biggin Hill formed part of the defensive ring around Kent and Sussex. They were used to attacking incoming aircraft often far from their base. The defence of their own station only began

BELOW A group of pilots from 79 Squadron at Biggin Hill in July 1940. The Hurricane squadron was posted north to recuperate and returned to Biggin Hill, the only squadron still to be operating from the battered station. On 8 September the squadron was posted away for a further rest.

RIGHT Entrants line up for the start of one of the Grosvenor Cup races at Lympne in the 1930s.

LYMPNE AIRPORT

The airport at Lympne in Kent, founded in 1916 as an emergency landing ground for Royal Flying Corps aircraft, played an important part during the Battle of Britain acting in a similar role for aircraft from the fighter stations in Kent and Sussex. Lympne became a civil airport in the interwar years, host to airmail aircraft and, from 1923, annual air races. The final race staged before the war was on 5 August 1939, by which time it had been requisitioned by the Royal Navy Fleet Air Arm. Though not a fighter station, it was heavily bombed on 15 August and temporarily put out of action. A raid on 30 August killed five local workmen. Fighters landed there only to refuel or in emergencies. Later in the war, Spitfires and Typhoons were stationed at Lympne for the war in Europe. Civil flying and racing was restored in 1946, but the airport finally ceased commercial flying in 1974.

BELOW The pilots stationed at Biggin Hill would relax in the White Hart pub in Brasted, Kent, near the Biggin Hill base. The board on which they all signed their names was still in existence after the war.

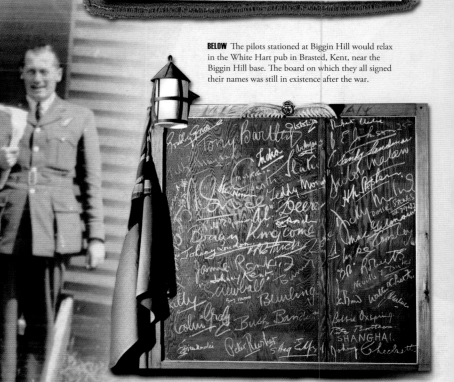

BELOW Spitfire spotter card.

SPITFIRE I (MERLIN)
Fighter
Span: 36' 10"   Length: 29' 11"   Height: 9' 3"

LEFT A visit to Biggin Hill by Lord Dowding, the former commander-in-chief of Fighter Command, in July 1951 to lay the foundation stone of the Biggin Hill Chapel, pictured below.

BELOW A German air force reconnaissance photograph of Manston airfield taken during the battle.

BELOW LEFT Spitfire and Hurricane replicas outside the RAF chapel at the Biggin Hill air base in 1966.

with an opening attack on 12 August, the day before "Eagle Day". The bombers attacked generally in small groups, often from low level, and were difficult to intercept or divert. The first attacks did limited damage, but the attacks on 15 and 18 August and two final devastating attacks on 30 August destroyed almost every building standing on the base. There was scant protection provided for the staff of the base but the number of dead was small except for the major attack on 30 August. Thirty-nine people were killed and 24 injured, including the only death among the almost 200 members of the Women's Auxiliary Air Force stationed at Biggin Hill. The exceptional heroism displayed by the WAAFs at Biggin Hill brought three of their number the award of the Military Medal. Only three more of these medals were awarded to WAAFs throughout the whole of the war.

Fighter Command had anticipated attacks against its airfields and mobile squads of labourers were directed to repair damage to the runways so that aircraft could continue to fly. The operations room was destroyed in one raid but an emergency operations room was set up in a local village shop so that the flow of information about incoming aircraft and instructions to the pilots could be maintained. The station staff and the pilots were housed in villages around the air base to avoid casualties, and every effort was made to conceal or camouflage the aircraft, remarkably few of which were ever destroyed on the ground.

During September, the heavy raids suddenly ceased with the switch to the bombing of London. In mid-September, a squadron of night fighters was posted to Biggin Hill to meet the challenge of German night bombing, but after three days it was transferred to Gatwick because of the difficulty of organizing two different sets

of operations from the same base. During September and October, the fighters at Biggin Hill continued to challenge the raids on London. So destroyed was the air base that there was little left for the enemy to attack, but it remained operational, the hub of an effective organization dispersed around the surrounding Kent countryside. In October and November, 92 Squadron and 74 Squadron, the latter commanded by "Sailor" Malan, engaged in regular dogfights with high-flying German intruders. On 30 November, two Spitfires took off without orders to try to shoot down the station's 600th enemy aircraft. A group of eight Me 109s was spotted near Deal and a straggler destroyed by the two Spitfires.

After the war, Biggin Hill was used by RAF Transport Command, but then again became a regular fighter base. In 1958, the station was closed, leaving an RAF Officer and Aircrew Selection Centre. This, too, was abandoned in 1992 and Biggin Hill became a fully civilian airport and the host for regular air shows.

RAF MANSTON

Manston, situated on the Isle of Thanet in Kent, was an RFC and RAF station from 1916 to 1999. It was the most heavily attacked air base during the Battle of Britain and was rendered unserviceable for six days and five nights between 14 August and 12 September, despite strenuous efforts by large mobile teams of workmen organized by the Air Ministry. Manston began life as an Admiralty aerodrome in 1915–16, but then became home to Royal Flying Corps aircraft defending against Zeppelins and Gotha bombers. At the start of the Second World War, it was a major Fighter Command base for 11 Group. Later in the war the airfield was used by aircraft testing Barnes Wallis's "bouncing bomb" and subsequently the first squadron of RAF Meteor jet fighters was based there. After the war, Manston was taken over by the United States air force as a base for fighters and fighter-bombers, but in 1961 the base returned to RAF use until its closure in 1999. It is now Kent International Airport.

LIEUTENANT GENERAL HANS-JÜRGEN STUMPFF (1889-1968)

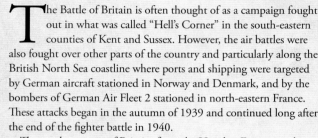

The commander chosen to lead the Norway-based Air Fleet 5 for attacks on British ports and shipping was a former Prussian army officer, Hans-Jürgen Stumpff. He was commissioned in the army in 1907 and served as a staff officer during the First World War. He stayed on in the small peacetime army and as a lieutenant colonel was made head of personnel in the secret German air force in 1933. He became air force chief of staff in 1937 in succession to Albert Kesselring. He held the post until January 1939 after which he held combat commands, first of Air Fleet 5, based in Scandinavia, then, from January 1944, as commander of the home defence of the Reich against the Combined Bomber Offensive. He was one of the three German signatories of the unconditional surrender of May 8 1945 in Berlin. Captured by the British, he was released in 1947.

The Battle of Britain is often thought of as a campaign fought out in what was called "Hell's Corner" in the south-eastern counties of Kent and Sussex. However, the air battles were also fought over other parts of the country and particularly along the British North Sea coastline where ports and shipping were targeted by German aircraft stationed in Norway and Denmark, and by the bombers of German Air Fleet 2 stationed in north-eastern France. These attacks began in the autumn of 1939 and continued long after the end of the fighter battle in 1940.

The northern areas of Britain, from the Humber Estuary to the Orkney Islands, which housed the Royal Navy's main base at Scapa Flow, were integrated into the overall defensive air plan, but were not strongly defended. The Home Chain radar stations were set up as far north as the Firth of Forth, while three divisions of anti-aircraft artillery defended the vulnerable port areas from the Humber to the Forth. A separate Orkney and Shetland Defence Area was also established, under the control of the Scottish-based 3rd Anti-Aircraft Division. The southern part of the region, from Lincolnshire to north Yorkshire, was defended by the aircraft of 12 Group, Fighter Command. Northern England and Scotland were defended by 13 Group. Plans were made to establish 14 Group to defend northern Scotland more effectively, but the organization could not be set up fully in time for the Battle of Britain. By early August, 12 Group had 14 squadrons while 13 Group had 13 squadrons, though only three of these had Spitfires.

Between the outbreak of war and the late summer of 1940, attacks on the area had been made by single aircraft or small groups of bombers which attacked the Humber area, Tyneside, Dundee and Aberdeen. For the German side, these were dangerous operations. Flown almost to the limit of range across wide areas of water, the prospects of finding targets with much accuracy were never good. Aircraft with battle damage or mechanical problems faced the prospect

BELOW The wreckage of one of the first two German aircraft shot down on British soil, a Heinkel He 111 bomber which crashed near Edinburgh in Scotland on 16 October 1939. The bombers were caught by two Spitfire squadrons as they attacked shipping in the Firth of Forth.

RIGHT German Junkers Ju 52 troop transport aircraft at an Oslo air base on 9 April 1940. The German invasion of Norway opened up the possibility of attacking targets in northern Britain from Scandinavian bases.

of crashing into a hostile sea long before they could reach land. When "Eagle Attack" was launched on 13 August, Air Fleet 5, stationed in Scandinavia, was expected to play its part in attacking northern Britain to tie down or destroy RAF forces, and to damage British trade and port facilities. On 15 August 1940, 100 aircraft from bases in Norway, made up of 65 Heinkel He 111 bombers and 35 Me 110s used to escort them, set off for an attack on the east coast around Tyneside and north Yorkshire. This proved to be the one major battle over northern Britain.

The fighters of 13 Group were alerted to the incoming force by radar and 72 Squadron's Spitfires were detailed to intercept over sea. The squadron was resting at Acklington after a gruelling few weeks at Biggin Hill. It met the German planes head on and forced the attackers to split up their forces. As the bombers reached the coastline, they were attacked by three further squadrons. The German aircraft inflicted no damage on airfields or factories, but destroyed 24 houses in Sunderland. They were harried the whole way, losing 15 aircraft, including 20 per cent of the Me 110s. A second attack by Junkers Ju 88 bombers stationed at Aalborg

in Denmark was more successful. They targeted the RAF bomber base at Driffield in Yorkshire, causing heavy damage. Though met by four squadrons from 12 Group, it proved impossible to prevent the bombers pressing home the attack. Some eight German aircraft were shot down. In both operations that day, Fighter Command lost none of its planes. So severe was the rate of loss for German forces that Air Fleet 5 suspended any further daytime attacks, vindicating Dowding's decision to establish the defensive air shield as far north as possible.

On the same date, 15 August, the German air force mounted a number of night raids against widely dispersed targets in Yorkshire and the north east of England. This set the pattern for the subsequent air battle in the north. Night raids, often by small numbers of bombers, were undertaken against ports and major cities throughout the region weeks before the onset of the Blitz against London in September. On 31 August, there was a destructive major raid against Liverpool. Although the fighter battle was confined to the major raids on 15 August, the north was never free of the air threat throughout the whole period of the Battle of Britain.

AIR VICE-MARSHAL RICHARD SAUL (1891-1965)

Richard Saul was the commander of 13 Group during the Battle of Britain, and later of 12 Group. He was born in Dublin and entered an army career in the Royal Army Service Corps. He joined the Royal Flying Corps and became a squadron commander by the end of the war. He was a keen sportsman and was RAF tennis champion twice, in 1928 and 1932. He was sent to Basra in Iraq in 1933 to command a squadron but returned to command 13 Group in 1939. He went on to command 12 Group and then the Eastern Mediterranean Air Defences. In June 1944, he retired from the RAF and became head of the UNRRA branch in the Balkans before moving to Rome as the vice chairman of the International Transport Commission. He left Rome in 1951 and became the manager of a university bookshop until retiring for good in 1959.

LEFT A rear gunner of a Boulton-Paul Defiant from 264 Squadron, taken on 9 August 1940 at the 12 Group station at Kirton-in-Lindsey, near the Humber Estuary. Attacks on northern England were to be repelled by aircraft from both 12 and 13 Groups.

ABOVE The result of one of many bombing raids on the port of Hull during 1940–41. Around 600 tons of bombs were dropped on the city during the Blitz. The first night raid took place on 24 August 1940 by aircraft stationed in France, but the heaviest bombing came later. Around 1,500 were killed in Hull by bombing during the war.

BELOW Hurricane aircraft from 111 Squadron being refuelled at the north Scottish base at Wick in April 1940. Aircraft in northern Scotland were intended to protect the Royal Navy and merchant convoys, and to supply photo reconnaissance of possible German invasion plans from Scandinavia.

CHURCHILL AND THE "FEW"

Winston Churchill's extraordinary reputation rests more than anything else on his defiant leadership of the British people during the Battle of Britain, a phrase that he himself first used on 18 June 1940 when he announced that the battle for France was over and "the battle of Britain is about to begin". At the very height of the battle, he famously told the House of Commons that the pilots of Fighter Command, the "few", were battling to save civilization for the many.

Churchill had always had an interest in air power and had helped to initiate long-distance bombing in 1914–15 by the Royal Naval Air Service against German airship bases. His understanding of the nature of air power was nevertheless unsophisticated and throughout the air battles of the summer of 1940, senior commanders battled to resist Churchill's demands to use up all available reserves regardless of the consequences. In May 1940, shortly after Churchill became prime minister, there developed a crisis over the supply of fighter aircraft to assist in the land battle in France. Churchill wanted to send as many squadrons as possible until finally persuaded on 19 May to agree to suspend any further transfers. High wastage continued however, and at a tense cabinet meeting on 3 June Dowding, using a graph showing the current loss rates of Hurricanes, made it clear to Churchill that the air battle in France would have to be ended in favour of conserving Fighter Command for the expected German assault.

Churchill was aware how much numbers counted and appointed Lord Beaverbrook to the new post of Minister of Aircraft Production to speed up the supply of fighters. He found it difficult to grasp the

BELOW Standing with the commander of British anti-aircraft defences, Sir Frederick Pile (left), Churchill looks anxiously at the sky during the air battles over London in September 1940.

RIGHT Churchill leaving No. 10 Downing Street. When he became prime minister on 10 May 1940, he later wrote that he felt he was "walking with destiny".

WINSTON CHURCHILL (1874-1965)

Winston Leonard Spencer Churchill was born into the Marlborough family, son of the Conservative politician, Lord Randolph Churchill. He was educated at Harrow and the army college at Sandhurst, and gained his first commission in the Queen's Own Hussars in 1895. He saw action in northern India and the Sudan before resigning his commission in 1899. He became a Conservative MP in 1900, switched to the Liberal Party in 1904 and back again to the Conservatives 20 years later. He achieved high office at a remarkably young age and by 1910 had been appointed Home Secretary, then a year later First Lord of the Admiralty. In the First World War he resigned over his handling of the campaign at Gallipoli, briefly served on the Western Front, then returned to Britain where he became Minister of Munitions in 1917. He was in and out of high office until 1929, but during the 1930s became an isolated backbencher, opposed to appeasement. In 1939, he was again appointed First Lord of the Admiralty and on 10 May 1940 became prime minister. Defeated at the 1945 election, he returned as prime minister in 1951 before retiring from political life in 1955.

LEFT On 28 August 1940, Churchill was driving to inspect defences in Kent when a Messerschmitt Me 109 crashed nearby at Church Whitfield outside Dover. Churchill ordered his car to stop and walked over to view the plane with his personal bodyguard Inspector W Thompson (right).

ABOVE Churchill in the cockpit of a Short biplane at Eastchurch on 29 November 1913. Churchill was an air power enthusiast from its inception just before the First World War.

effort needed to accelerate production and was impatient for instant results. In mid-August 1940, he demanded of the Air Minister, Sir Archibald Sinclair, why the 1,600 pilots assigned to staff duties and the 2,000 pilots involved in training were not in the skies resisting the Germans, and had to be persuaded that many were well over age or essential to keeping up the supply of trained pilots. Throughout the battle, Churchill insisted on being supplied with regular reports of the number of available aircraft and pilots each day.

It was at the high point of the battle that Churchill made his famous "few" speech, on 20 August 1940. A few days earlier he had visited the headquarters of 11 Group and had been heard to mutter to himself in the car afterwards the most memorable phrase of his speech: "Never in the field of human conflict was so much owed by so many to so few." The speech was made in the House of Commons, where a small audience gave it little attention. Churchill said three times as much about Bomber Command as he did about the fighter squadrons. The impact came with the wider public, who grasped the notion that Fighter Command was playing David to Germany's Goliath, and found in the concept of "the few" a fitting testament to British heroism.

By coincidence, Churchill was also present at Park's headquarters in Uxbridge on 15 September, the day later remembered as Battle of Britain Day. On that morning

Churchill watched as Park ordered his squadrons into service. As more aircraft were scrambled Churchill asked Park what reserves there were and received the reply, "There are none". Churchill interpreted this as evidence that the force was close to crisis, though Park had only intended to indicate that all his squadrons were currently operational and needed the additional support of 12 Group. The experience left a sombre impact on Churchill which was reflected in the account of the battle in his later history of the war. The experience of the Blitz also had a profound impression on Churchill's outlook. The relative failure of the night air defences against German bombers provoked a crisis at the Air Ministry which resulted in pressure to remove Dowding from command, and although he had long admired him, Churchill in the end made no effort to save Dowding when he was finally transferred in November 1940.

Churchill's role in the summer and autumn of 1940 was not primarily to assist with the practical problems in winning the Battle of Britain, but to rally popular support for the continuation of the war, and to provide the public with evidence of British defiance and fortitude in the face of a brutal enemy. Even though the numbers of air crew and fighters available were almost always higher than the number of German fighter pilots and crew, Churchill also succeeded in cementing in the popular memory of the battle the idea that it was won by the few.

LORD BEAVERBROOK (1879–1964)

A close friend of Churchill, William Maxwell Aitken was a leading newspaper proprietor and staunch Conservative politician. He was born in Canada, where he made his fortune, and then moved to Britain where he became an MP in 1910. During the First World War, he bought the *Daily Express* and two years later launched the *Sunday Express*. He was created Lord Beaverbrook in 1917. In 1923 he added the *Evening Standard* to his list of papers. He served as Minister of Information in 1918 but did not achieve high political office again until Churchill made him Minister of Aircraft Production in 1940 before the onset of the Battle of Britain. He succeeded in speeding up fighter output at the cost of the wider aircraft production programmes. In 1941, he was moved to the Ministry of Supply and between 1943 and 1945 was Lord Privy Seal. His son served in the so-called "Millionaires' Squadron" during the battle.

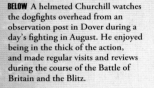

BELOW A helmeted Churchill watches the dogfights overhead from an observation post in Dover during a day's fighting in August. He enjoyed being in the thick of the action, and made regular visits and reviews during the course of the Battle of Britain and the Blitz.

LEFT Churchill visits the aftermath of a heavy bomb attack on the London borough of Battersea on 10 September 1940. It was the sight of the ruins in London that inspired in him a strong wish for vengeance against the German enemy.

THE PILOTS

The life of a pilot during the Battle of Britain had much in common on both sides of the conflict. Both air forces were an elite, more highly trained than almost any other units in the armed forces. Compared with an army, the numbers involved in flying and fighting during the Battle of Britain were tiny. The squadron organization put together small numbers of men who had to work as a team to be successful. Losses of squadron members made it necessary to create a system where newcomers could be integrated into established fighting units. Pilots could regard themselves as special, but the harsh reality of combat was a high rate of death and disablement.

The German air force in 1939 had a larger and more sophisticated system of pilot recruitment and training than any other European force. There were an estimated 50,000 aircrew available when war broke out, trained in a total of 100 training schools. The British system was much smaller but was expanding rapidly in 1939, and became capable by the time of the battle of supplying more fighter pilots per week than the German air force. The pattern of training was similar, though German pilots had many more flying hours, including 150 on basic flying training and a further 50 specialized in flying on the

aircraft they would fly in combat. The German Flying Training Regiment was the equivalent of the British Initial Training Wing. Here pilots were familiarized with military life. There followed actual flying training in elementary flying training schools in Germany. Similar schools in Britain were supplemented from April 1940 onwards by the creation of the British Empire Air Training Scheme, agreed between the countries of the British Commonwealth at Ottawa in December 1939. By its peak in 1942, the scheme could turn out 28,000 aircrew per year. Most of the RAF crew trained abroad came from schools in Southern Rhodesia, South Africa and Canada.

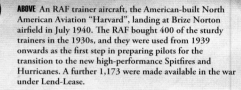

ABOVE An RAF trainer aircraft, the American-built North American Aviation "Harvard", landing at Brize Norton airfield in July 1940. The RAF bought 400 of the sturdy trainers in the 1930s, and they were used from 1939 onwards as the first step in preparing pilots for the transition to the new high-performance Spitfires and Hurricanes. A further 1,173 were made available in the war under Lend-Lease.

BELOW The crew of a Hurricane aircraft camp out in a caravan on the airfield awaiting the call to scramble in April 1940.

RIGHT Pilots of 504 Squadron outside the White Hart Inn, Brasted in Kent. The Hurricane squadron was stationed in Scotland at the start of the battle but was moved south during August.

GROUP CAPTAIN ADOLPH "SAILOR" MALAN (1910–1963)

Adolph Malan became one of the most successful of Britain's air aces during the Second World War. Born in Cape Province, South Africa, Malan joined the South African navy as a cadet in 1924, which explains the nickname "Sailor" later used by his RAF colleagues. He learned to fly in early 1935, and then joined the RAF in March. He was a flight lieutenant flying Spitfires when war came in 1939. During the Battle of Britain he was acting squadron leader of 74 Squadron at Biggin Hill where he established his reputation as a cool and effective flyer, and an excellent shot. He was retired from operations in August 1941 by which time he had been attributed 27 "kills". He later commanded a Free French Fighter Wing over the D-Day landings. When he returned to South Africa after the war, he helped to lead the widespread protests against the implementation of apartheid. He died in 1963 of Parkinson's disease.

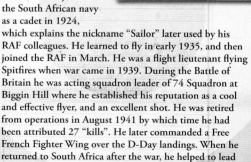

BELOW A dead German airman in the wreckage of his Junkers Ju 87B dive-bomber brought down over Sussex in August 1940. German pilot losses escalated dramatically during August and September, and included many experienced crew trained in the 1930s.

MIDDLE German airmen at a German flying school in Hanover undergo instruction in navigation during the war. Standards of navigation were high, maximising the impact that German air forces had in attacks on British targets.

With the coming of war, basic training was supplemented by an intermediate stage of combat training on the aircraft that a pilot was destined to fly. In 1939, operational training schools were set up in Germany and operational training units in Britain. These units took some of the aircraft and skilled pilots needed on the aerial front line, but it was essential that pilots should become familiar with an aircraft and with the principles of air combat before having to fight. In Britain, the need to speed up the supply of pilots led to the creation of so-called "C" squadrons made up of five or six experienced pilots, whose job it was to introduce newcomers quickly to actual combat in relatively safe areas of the country before being posted to south-east England. In general, German pilots enjoyed more thorough training and a longer period of pre-combat flying, which explains their higher kill ratios in battle and their better survival rate.

The Battle of Britain was fought by around 2,000 British and German fighter pilots, while there were around 1,500 bomber pilots in the German air fleets. The German fighter force never had as many pilots on hand as the RAF, averaging 66 per cent of British strength in the weeks of the battle, and sinking to only 50 per cent by November 1940. During August, British operational training units were turning out 320 fighter pilots a month, though casualties reached 22 per cent of the force. The greatest pressure felt on the British side was the shortage of trained ground staff and technicians, both areas where the German air force was better supplied. The one advantage enjoyed by RAF pilots was to fight over home territory. German pilots were lost to the force once they had crash-landed or baled out. In September, the loss rate for the German fighter force rose to over 23 per cent; during the whole course of the battle 967 German aircrew were made prisoners-of-war, while 638 bodies were identified. In contrast, many British airmen who baled out over England found themselves flying

LEFT A Defiant spotter card.

DEFIANT (MERLIN)
Fighter
Span: 39' 4" Length: 35' 4" Height: 12' 2"

again the same day in a new aircraft. Those with light wounds could be flying again after a few days.

High rates of casualty and the sheer pressure of fighting over and over again made the pilots' lives particularly arduous. Badly mauled or tired squadrons were withdrawn to recuperate while new squadrons took their place. Those in combat spent hours waiting for the order to scramble to their aircraft and then endured anything from several hours to a few minutes of dangerous flying and combat; after the end of the day's fighting, pilots found themselves in the peculiar position of once again being part of the local civilian community in bars and clubs, and churches. The element of daredevil was never very far from the daily experience of a pilot, caught between the normality of life on base or in the nearby towns and villages, and the knowledge that only his own skill, daring and luck might ensure that he returned the following day. Aerial combat has often been compared with medieval warfare with its emphasis on chivalry and individual prowess and the many memoirs and diaries of pilots who fought through the battle show that this comparison is not altogether unfounded.

BELOW A group of German pilots with their dogs stand in front of a fighter aircraft at an air base facing the Channel coast in the summer of 1940. Pilots on both sides showed the same strong sense of camaraderie, superstition and courage.

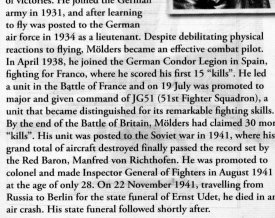
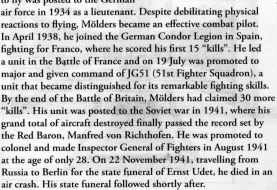

COLONEL WERNER MÖLDERS (1913–1941)

The most famous German air ace of the Second World War, Werner Mölders claimed 100 enemy aircraft destroyed as his remarkable tally of victories. He joined the German army in 1931, and after learning to fly was posted to the German air force in 1934 as a lieutenant. Despite debilitating physical reactions to flying, Mölders became an effective combat pilot. In April 1938, he joined the German Condor Legion in Spain, fighting for Franco, where he scored his first 15 "kills". He led a unit in the Battle of France and on 19 July was promoted to major and given command of JG51 (51st Fighter Squadron), a unit that became distinguished for its remarkable fighting skills. By the end of the Battle of Britain, Mölders had claimed 30 more "kills". His unit was posted to the Soviet war in 1941, where his grand total of aircraft destroyed finally passed the record set by the Red Baron, Manfred von Richthofen. He was promoted to colonel and made Inspector General of Fighters in August 1941 at the age of only 28. On 22 November 1941, travelling from Russia to Berlin for the state funeral of Ernst Udet, he died in an air crash. His state funeral followed shortly after.

THE COMMANDERS

The Battle of Britain produced a confrontation between air commanders of the highest quality. On the British side, Air Vice-Marshal Keith Park, a New Zealander who came to Britain in 1916, played a central part in devising a set of tactics which would maximize the impact that his force might have on the enemy. On the German side, the two main air fleet commanders, Field Marshal Albert Kesselring and Field Marshal Hugo Sperrle – both promoted to their rank by a grateful Hitler in July 1940 after the defeat of France – also developed flexible tactical approaches to the battle as it unfolded over the summer of 1940.

The German side nevertheless laboured under a large disadvantage. The conduct of operations by Kesselring's Air Fleet 2 and Sperrle's Air Fleet 3 was overseen by the German air force commander-in-chief, Hermann Goering. His interventions, often prompted by discussions with Hitler, seldom bore much relation to reality on the battlefield.

BELOW Erhard Milch (far right), the former director of Lufthansa and state secretary in the German Air Ministry, at RAF Mildenhall whilst on an official visit in 1937. He was shown the British "shadow" aircraft factories and was impressed by what he saw, but he was resented by Goering and excluded from much decision-making in the years before the outbreak of war.

RIGHT A festival for the aviation sector of the Hitler Youth at the German Air Ministry on 1 April 1940. The grandiose building was constructed on Leipzigerstrasse in Berlin and is still used today as ministerial offices.

Although Kesselring and Sperrle were allowed to argue over issues where they thought strategic choices were wrong, they had little hope of overturning a decision once Goering had made it. The best example of this was the choice made in early September to switch to attacks on London. Sperrle, who had commanded the German Condor Legion during the Spanish Civil War, understood well enough that Fighter Command had not been defeated. He wanted to continue to concentrate German efforts on destroying Fighter Command's capacity to inflict damage by means of attacks on airfields and radar stations. Kesselring, on the other hand, assumed that decisive combat with Fighter Command could only be achieved by luring RAF fighters up into the air and then defeating them in open battle with German fighters. Since the information available to Goering suggested that Fighter Command was close to exhaustion, he opted for the argument that London should now be the target. This also satisfied Hitler's demand that since Berlin was being targeted by the Allies, any immunity for London should be removed.

Throughout the battle, Sperrle and Kesselring sought ways to engage Fighter Command in unequal combat. They used diversionary attacks, operations only using large numbers of fighters and regular flights over the Channel to tempt British fighters over water (something that was prohibited by Park). Some of the losses inflicted on Fighter Command were due to these tactical adjustments. Yet for German commanders, however well they understood the tactical dimensions of the effort

AIR CHIEF MARSHAL SIR KEITH PARK
(1892–1975)

Keith Park was born in New Zealand, the son of a geologist. He saw service as an artilleryman during the First World War, first in the ANZAC landings at Gallipoli, then in the Battle of the Somme. Wounded in France, he joined the Royal Flying Corps in December 1916. He became something of an air ace and ended the war as a major commanding 48 Squadron. He remained in the post-war RAF and in 1938 became one of Dowding's staff officers. He took command of 11 Group as an air vice-marshal in April 1940, but was posted away to Training Command later in the year. In January 1942, he went to Egypt as the local air commander, and then oversaw the air defence of Malta in the summer of 1942. He ended the war as Allied Air Forces Commander-in-Chief, South East Asia. After promotion to air chief marshal, he returned to New Zealand in 1946 where he took part in local politics until his retirement.

to win air superiority, the overall problem was the requirement laid down in regular directives from Hitler and from Goering to attack a wide variety of dispersed targets with a force of medium bombers and fighters at the limit of their operational range.

Park had a difficult task in the face of the large numbers of German aircraft and the certainty that his Group would bear the brunt of the air assault. He was a clear-sighted and organized manager of the battlefield, and he was fortunate in suffering much less intervention from on high than his German counterparts. Park's most important tactical priority was to ensure that squadrons attacked or defended in pairs, allowing enough strength to inflict damage on the enemy, but not exposing too much of the force to German counter-attack at any one time. This choice meant that Fighter Command took a high rate of casualty, with squadrons often fighting against larger numbers. It also meant that a wide number of targets could be defended and that the approaching bombers would understand that even if they evaded one series of attacks, they would be subject to more over the course of their long and dangerous round trip. Park was also successful in September in persuading Dowding to send all the pilots with good combat experience to fight in south-east England, leaving the less imperilled squadrons further north and west to cope with inexperienced personnel. Yet for all his successes in adapting his force swiftly to new developments in the height of battle, he suffered regular criticism from other senior airmen who thought they could fight it better. In

ABOVE A meeting of the British Air Council in March 1941. The council was the governing body of the RAF, and included serving air commanders and politicians. In the centre sit the air minister, Sir Archibald Sinclair and the RAF chief of staff, Sir Charles Portal (right).

November 1940, he was abruptly told that he was to be relieved of his command. Hugo Sperrle, on the other hand, was kept in place in northern France throughout the four years leading to the Normandy invasion in June 1944, when he had the final ignominy of trying to combat Eisenhower's 12,000 aircraft with the 170 aircraft still left to him to defend the coast of France.

FIELD MARSHAL ALBERT KESSELRING (1885–1960)

One of the most successful air commanders of the Second World War, Albert Kesselring was one of of many young army officers who converted to the German air force when it was created in 1933. He was born in Bavaria and served in staff positions in the First World War. In 1933, he was appointed to run the administrative office of the newly founded Air Ministry and learned to fly at the age of 48 in order to understand his task better. In 1936, he became air force chief of staff, and in 1938 commander of the First Air Fleet. He led the Second Air Fleet in the Battle of France, for which he was promoted to field marshal. He continued to command his fleet during the Battle of Britain and later in the invasion of the Soviet Union, but was then posted as Commander-in-Chief South to try to stabilize the campaign in the Mediterranean. He led German forces in the Italian campaign, and then took over command in north-west Europe in March 1945. In 1947, he was condemned to death for ordering reprisals in Italy, but the sentence was commuted to life imprisonment and he was released in 1952 in poor health.

LEFT German air force commanders in dress uniform at a reception held in Hitler's office on 4 September 1940. To Hitler's left stand Hermann Goering and Albert Kesselring, commander of Air Fleet 2. To his right are Hugo Sperrle, commander of Air Fleet 3, and Erhard Milch, state secretary of the Air Ministry.

AMERICANS IN FIGHTER COMMAND

Among the large number of non-British pilots who flew in the Battle of Britain were eight Americans who had volunteered to fly aircraft on the Allied side. They risked a great deal since they violated the American Neutrality Legislation of 1937. The penalty for fighting for a-- belligerent power was loss of US citizenship, a fine of $10,000 and a possible prison sentence. They were almost all of them enthusiastic flyers who wanted to do something more than perform air stunts or fly freight.

A number of the volunteers were recruited by the American mercenary Charles Sweeny, whose network of contacts in the United States and Canada was used to supply false papers and money for potential recruits to the French air force. Another recruiting agency, the Clayton Knight Committee, supplied over 8,000 pilots to serve with the Royal Canadian Air Force and the RAF. Though many later flew from British bases, none of them served in the Battle of Britain.

Three of the Americans who did fight in 1940 – Eugene Tobin, Andrew Mamedoff and Vernon "Shorty" Keough (who was only 1.47 metres (4ft 10in) high – were sent to France by Sweeny, arriving in early June 1940 just as French resistance to the German invasion was crumbling. They fled south away from the German army and managed to board the last refugee boat to leave France for England on 23 June.

In Britain, the three Americans, with the help of sympathetic MPs and influential Americans living in London, joined the RAF. They were sent for training in July and on 16 August they were posted to the 11 Group fighter station at Middle Wallop to join 609 Squadron. That same day the first American to join Fighter Command, the American Olympic bobsleigh gold medallist Billy Fiske, was shot down. Fiske had spent much of his time in Britain before the war and had numerous friends in British high society. He joined the RAF on 18 September 1939 and was posted in July 1940 to 601 (Auxiliary) Squadron, also known as the "Millionaires' Squadron" because of the wealthy society men who had first formed it. Fiske was a popular and skilful pilot but on 16 August a German Ju 87 dive-bomber succeeded in setting the reserve fuel tank of his Hurricane alight. Fiske refused to bale out and flew his plane back, badly burned. He died of his injuries the following day.

GENERAL CARL "TOOEY" SPAATZ (1891–1974)

General Spaatz (above centre) was the commander of the US 8th Air Force in Britain in 1942. He was chosen to go to Britain two years earlier, in 1940, as an observer of the Battle of Britain. He was a career airman, first seeing action on the US-Mexican border in 1916 and again in France at the end of the First World War. He served in various command and staff positions in the interwar years, and in November 1940 became Chief of the Plans Division of the US Air Corps. After serving in Britain in 1942 he was sent to the Mediterranean as commander of Allied Air Forces under Eisenhower. In December 1943 he was also appointed commander-in-chief of all US Strategic Air Forces in Europe. After the war he became the first chief of staff of the newly formed US Air Force in September 1947. He retired from the service in 1948.

BELOW A group of pilots from the all-American 71 "Eagle" Squadron, formed in September 1940. There were three all-American squadrons until they were finally absorbed into the British-based US Army Air Forces later in the war.

BELOW RIGHT Bobby Fiske, the American Olympic bobsleigh champion, in RAF uniform in 1940.

BELOW RIGHT Three of the Americans who served in the Battle of Britain. From left to right, Eugene Tobin, Vernon Keough and Andrew Mamedoff. Keough was less than five feet in height and was affectionately known as "Shorty".

A second casualty in August was a young American airman, Arthur Donahue. He had made his way from Minnesota via Canada to London in June 1940. He was signed up by the RAF, and joined 12 Group's 64 Squadron on 3 August 1940. Nine days later he was hit by an Me 109 and although able to return to base, he was badly burned. He survived, but did not see action again until the battle was over. Three other Americans flew during the battle: John Haviland, who lived in Britain before the war, was posted to 151 Squadron but crashed his Hurricane in training and saw no combat during the battle; Phillip Lekrone came via Canada in July and was posted to 616 squadron in September, but flew only one combat mission during the battle; the last was Hugh Reilley, who posed as a Canadian to gain entry, and was posted to 66 Squadron on 17 September. Reilley was shot down by the German air ace Werner Mölders on 17 October. Of all the pilots who joined during the Battle of Britain, only Haviland survived the war.

The American presence was eventually acknowledged by Winston Churchill who agreed to a suggestion from Sweeny's nephew that a separate squadron should be established for American pilots. The Eagle Squadron, No 71, was activated in mid-September 1940, one of three eventually formed before all American units were absorbed in September 1942 into the US Army Air Forces 4th Fighter Group. Both the British and American governments turned a blind eye to the violation of the neutrality legislation. During the summer of 1940, a delegation of leading American airmen, including the future overall commander of US air forces in Europe, Carl Spaatz, and the US fighter ace from the First World War, Lieutenant Colonel Frank Hunter, was sent to Britain to observe and report on the air battle. Spaatz told the chief of the Air Corps, Henry Arnold, that in his view the Germans' chance of destroying the RAF was "not particularly good". A second delegation sent in October reported that "the Germans have been definitely defeated in day fighting". American commanders drew important lessons from the battle for the future conduct of US air operations after Pearl Harbor.

LEFT The chief of the US Army Air Corps, Henry "Hap" Arnold (left), and William Knudsen, the Danish-American car manufacturer and head of the Office for Production Management (right), inspect an American aircraft factory. By the time of the Battle of Britain, a regular flow of aircraft was crossing the Atlantic to meet British needs.

THE SWEENYS

Two Americans, an uncle (above right) and nephew both called Charles Sweeny, played an important part in recruiting American citizens to come to Britain and join the RAF in the summer of 1940. The older man, a famous American mercenary who had twice been expelled from West Point, served in the French Foreign Legion during the First World War (where he won the rank of colonel), and then fought regularly in the interwar years, including a spell on the side of Spanish republicans in the civil war. Colonel Sweeny recruited American pilots in the United States to fight for Finland against the Soviet Union, then to fight for France against Germany. Some of his pilots ended up in Britain in June 1940 where his nephew, who was an influential businessman and socialite in London, persuaded the RAF to take on American airmen in designated squadrons. The Eagle Squadrons were the result and Charles Jnr succeeded in getting the RAF to make his flamboyant uncle an honorary Group Captain of 71 Squadron in 1940.

BELOW A group of pilots from the American "Flying Tigers", volunteers who helped Chiang Kai-shek's Nationalist forces in southern China during the Sino-Japanese war, c.1940. American volunteers were to be found wherever there was air combat even though the United States was formally a neutral country.

ALLIES IN FIGHTER COMMAND

RAF SQUADRON 303 (POLISH)

One of the Polish squadrons formed during the Battle of Britain was 303 "Kościuszko" Squadron, named after the eighteenth-century Polish hero General Tadeusz Kościuszko. It was formed on 2 August 1940 at Northolt, and became operational at the end of the month with 21 Polish pilots and 135 Polish ground staff, together with RAF commanders to familiarize the crews with Fighter Command requirements. By the time it was withdrawn to rest on 11 October, the squadron claimed the highest number of kills of all RAF squadrons. The 126 claimed was almost certainly an exaggeration though subsequent research has shown at least 44, the highest number for any Hurricane squadron. It maintained its high scoring record in operations over France in 1941–43 and came top in a gunnery competition organized in 11 Group. It remained based in Britain for the rest of the war and was the most successful of the Polish squadrons. Its pilots were the only Poles invited to the victory parade in London, but they refused to attend because other Polish units were not included. The unit was disbanded in December 1946.

Although the large majority of pilots in the Battle of Britain were British, around one-fifth came from Commonwealth countries and from the air forces of nations already conquered by German armies by the summer of 1940. The air effort was genuinely international and became more so as the war went on.

The largest number from overseas came from New Zealand, including the commander of 11 Group himself, Keith Park. Some 127 took part in the battle, many of them volunteers from before the war. There were 30 Australians, who also joined before the outbreak of war. Most of the more than 100 Canadian pilots also arrived pre-war in order to get the opportunity to fly, the motive which had brought most of the volunteers from Australia and New Zealand. In June 1940, the Canadian air force also sent a squadron of Hurricanes to join the defence of Britain and 1 Squadron, RCAF, saw action with 11 Group from 18 August, flying out of Northolt. It was renumbered 401 Squadron in March 1941 to avoid confusion with the RAF's own 1 Squadron. There were also 27 pilots from southern Africa who came to Britain rather than fight with the South African Air Forces. In 1939, the Rhodesians also gave a "gift squadron", No 266, which fought in Spitfires during the battle.

ABOVE Canadian airmen boarding trains at Ottawa on 8 March 1940 at the start of a long Transatlantic journey to serve in the RAF. Eventually thousands of Canadians flew in Fighter and Bomber Command, or in units of the Royal Canadian Air Force.

BELOW Shoulder badge worn by Canadian pilots who flew in the Battle of Britain.

ABOVE LEFT Polish pilots from 303 Squadron meet the Air Minister, Sir Archibald Sinclair in October 1940. The Polish squadrons had among the highest "scores" of any in Fighter Command.

BELOW Trainee French pilots in Britain during a parade salute the French flag. The Free French forces were constituted by Charles de Gaulle in August 1940, but only a handful of French pilots actually saw combat during the Battle.

The Commonwealth pilots had none of the problems faced by the European crewmen who wanted to be integrated into Fighter Command, partly because they shared a common language and partly because they had generally been trained in the RAF. The largest contingents from Europe were the Poles and the Czechs, who arrived by a number of routes from the occupation of their countries. By June, there were around 1,500 Poles undergoing training. Problems of language and discipline dogged the training programme, but many of the Polish pilots were already highly trained and demonstrably fearless. Churchill was keen to make use of them and in early July the British cabinet approved the formation of Polish squadrons, though they were in general to be commanded by RAF officers. At least 146 Poles saw action in the Battle of Britain, organized in two squadrons, numbers 302 and 303, or scattered among British squadrons. The Polish air force squadrons were formed in July and August 1940 and both saw combat during the battle, achieving a high ratio of kills to losses.

There were also 88 Czechs serving in Fighter Command, and many others who did ground staff duties at Fighter Command stations. The Czechs were also allowed to form two squadrons in July 1940, numbers 310 and 312, both at Duxford flying Hurricanes, but 312 Squadron was then sent north to defend Merseyside while 310 Squadron fought over southern Britain. In addition there were 14 French pilots, though the first all-French squadron, No. 341 "Alsace", was not formed until 1943. In summer 1940, there were about 500 French aircrew in Britain. They were used to form the core of the Free French Air Forces. Only a handful took part in the battle, organized in a mixed Anglo-French squadron stationed at Odiham in Hampshire. The rest were organized in forces designed to operate under the orders of Charles de Gaulle, leader of the Free French forces, and later saw service in Africa.

The contribution of the non-British airmen who fought in the Battle of Britain has seldom been acknowledged fully, but many of their names can be read on the monuments to those who died in the battle. Their motives were mixed. Some joined from a love of flying, some from a hatred of Hitlerism. There was never any question about their quality as pilots and they provided a much-needed core of skilled airmen at a critical point in Britain's war effort.

RAF SQUADRON 310 (CZECH)

The first Czechoslovak Squadron was formed at Duxford on 10 July 1940 flying Hurricanes and was operational by 18 August. It was the first squadron to be manned by foreign pilots, but was commanded by an RAF officer, Squadron Leader Douglas Blackwood. It operated with 12 Group throughout the battle and claimed 37.5 victories. In 1941, it flew fighter sweeps over the Channel and in October 1941 re-equipped with Spitfires. It was then based in Cornwall until 1943 and in 1944 was converted to a fighter-bomber role with the Spitfire IX for the invasion of Normandy. In August 1945, it was flown to Hildesheim in Germany and then on to Prague where it became part of a new Czech air force. It was formally disbanded in February 1946.

ABOVE RIGHT Two Polish pilots pose with their Hurricane fighter. Despite initial distrust by the authorities, Polish pilots proved to be skilled and fearless in combat, and were allowed to form two squadrons of their own during the Battle of Britain.

BELOW Pilots from Australia, New Zealand and Canada arriving in Britain at the height of the Blitz. Commonwealth crew undertook their initial training in air training schools set up in their own countries and completed operational flying training at British-based training units.

RIGHT Shoulder badge worn by Australian members of the RAF. By September 1940 Fighter Command had become a multinational force.

BELOW Shoulder badge worn by New Zealanders who flew in the Battle. New Zealand provided the largest number of overseas pilots, 127 in all, including Air Chief-Marshal Keith Park.

RIGHT The badge awarded to Czechoslovak pilots on qualification. Squadrons 310 and 312 were Czech fighter sqadrons although the top scoring Czech Battle of Britain Ace, Sergeant Josef Frantisek, flew with the Polish 303 Squadron. He gained 17 "victories" in 28 days.

THE BOMBING OF LONDON
◎ 7 SEPTEMBER 1940

The first day of the "Blitz" is usually taken to be 7 September 1940. Bombing of ports and towns outside London had been going on since July, but the first major operation against the capital – and the largest operation of its kind yet mounted by the German air force during the battle – marked a decisive shift in German strategy.

This change has often been attributed to Hitler's anger at a series of RAF raids mounted against Berlin from the night of 25–26 August. On 4 September in a speech to the German parliament, Hitler promised that he would erase British cities in retaliation. But the shift to city bombing had been foreseen in German air force planning once Fighter Command was regarded as close to defeat. Poor intelligence assessments persuaded Goering that the British fighter force was close to extinction and the shift to bombing major ports and industrial cities inland (particularly aircraft industry targets) had already occurred several weeks before Hitler's speech, with heavy attacks on Bristol, Liverpool and Birmingham. On 2 September, Goering ordered heavy attacks

on London to begin, and on 5 September they were finally approved by Hitler. The object was now to try to undermine the British war economy, continue the pressure of the blockade and perhaps break the British will to continue the war. That day Goering arrived at Cap Gris Nez to discuss the new campaign with his commanders and, famously, to be photographed staring at the White Cliffs of Dover through binoculars. He told air force leaders that the attack would produce a decisive effect, perhaps within only a few days.

None of this change was yet evident to the British side. On 7 September, Londoners basked in exceptional autumn temperatures, expecting the air battle to continue against more distant RAF targets. Park was absent from his headquarters on a visit to Bentley Priory. His squadrons and those of 10 and 12 Groups were on standby to expect further attacks on fighter stations. When, at a little before 4 p.m., radar warnings arrived of a substantial force approaching over the Channel, it was assumed that their destination was an attack on Fighter Command. The squadrons airborne were thus positioned to defend airfields, and

GENERAL SIR FREDERICK PILE (1884–1976)

A career soldier who joined the British army in 1902 and served in the Royal Artillery throughout the First World War, Frederick Pile had the responsibility of organizing the anti-aircraft artillery for the Battle of Britain. He joined the Royal Tank Corps in the 1920s and later served in Egypt from 1932 to 1936. The following year he was made a major general and posted to command the 1st Anti-Aircraft Division guarding London. In 1939, he became Commander-in-Chief Anti-Aircraft Command, a post he held throughout the war. After the war, he became Director-General of Housing, Ministry of Works, helping to rebuild the cities his guns had earlier defended.

LEFT A group of bombed-out survivors of the attacks on Croydon airport and its surroundings on 7 September 1940.

BELOW LEFT King George VI (third from left) visiting the East End of London the day after the heavy attacks of 7–8 September. A few days later the first bomb fell on Buckingham Palace.

BELOW German ground crew load bombs onto a Heinkel He 111 during the daylight attacks on British cities. During the course of the battle more incendiaries were used as German commanders realized how much more damage could be done by fire.

ABOVE Brigadier General Sir Frederick Pile with an anti-aircraft gun crew in December 1942.

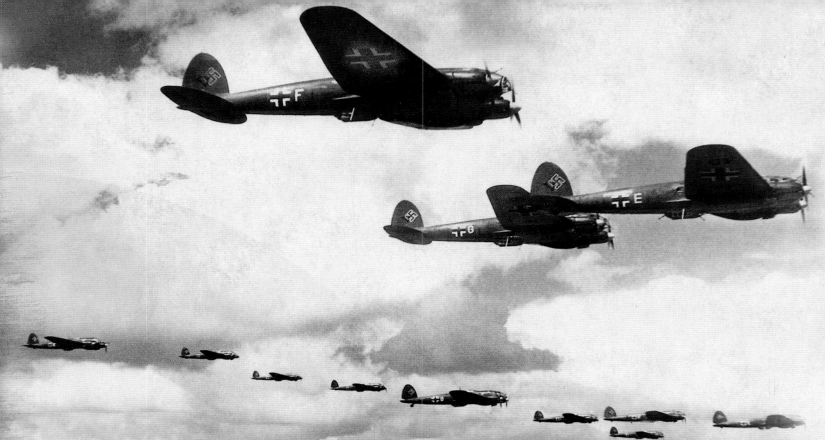

ABOVE A group of Berliners look at damage done by an RAF Bomber Command raid on 4 October 1940. Although British attacks were small when compared with the Blitz, the operations were designed to demonstrate to the German public that they had no immunity from bomb attack.

not to attack a major bomber stream heading for London. The first wave of attack consisted of 348 bombers escorted for the first time by a large part of the fighter force, 617 Me 109s and Me 110s. So large was the fighter force that when Fighter Command eventually got 23 squadrons into the air, they were forced to fight the German fighter screen rather than penetrate to the bombers. The bombers fanned out and attacked the area around the Royal Arsenal at Woolwich, the docks at West Ham and other docks and oil targets along the Thames. Most bombers got through to deliver their load of around 300 tons. The German side lost 40 aircraft, but 28 RAF fighters were lost, 16 heavily damaged and 17 pilots killed or seriously wounded.

At 8 p.m., a second wave of around 300 bombers attacked again, guided by the large fires burning throughout the dockland area. The first bombs dropped on Battersea, where the power station was put out of action. Little could be done to attack the bombers and many of the 264 anti-aircraft guns defending the capital were in the wrong place to engage major raids on central London. German bombers roamed over the capital until 4 a.m. the following morning. A further 330 tons of bombs were dropped and 440 incendiary canisters. A total of 436 Londoners were killed. Churchill himself came to view the damage the following day. On 11 September, he broadcast to the nation London's resolve to continue "taking it". By that time, over 1,000 Londoners had been killed in the day and night raids since 7 September.

TOP A large group of Heinkel He 111 medium-bombers in a training flight near the English coast in the autumn of 1940. They were obsolescent by 1940 and carried only a small bombload of around 900 kg (2,000 pounds).

ABOVE British firemen leaving a water-soaked building after fighting fires started during the 10 hours of German bombing on the night of 7–8 September 1940.

JUNKERS JU 88 BOMBER

The Junkers medium bomber became the mainstay of the German bomber force during the Second World War and was also converted to a major role as a night-fighter against the threat of Allied bombing of Germany. Over the course of the war, over 15,000 were produced. The bomber was designed in 1936 by the Hugo Junkers company in Dessau and it first flew on 21 December 1936. Its high speed was then undermined by insistence from the air force technical office that it should be capable of diving and by the decision to install on-board armament. Technical problems delayed its introduction; only 12 were ready by the time war broke out and too few were available for the Battle of Britain and the Blitz. The night-fighter version was introduced into service in July 1940. The aircraft was vulnerable to fast modern fighters and 313 were destroyed between July and October 1940, but it later became the backbone of the bomber force as well as a versatile heavy fighter, torpedo-bomber, dive-bomber and reconnaissance aircraft. In all, some 44 major variants were produced. The bomber version carried a crew of four and a maximum of 3,600 kg (8,000 pounds) of bombs.

BATTLE OF BRITAIN DAY
⊙ 15 SEPTEMBER 1940

The air battles over southern England on 15 September 1940 have long been commemorated as Battle of Britain Day. At the time it was believed that 185 German aircraft had been destroyed in a single day, the largest victory of any day of the battle. Only after the war was it learned that the true figure was just one-third of the number. This nevertheless represented a heavy loss for the German side at a time when its leadership was still hoping that the RAF would be defeated in a matter of days. The day symbolized the terms of the conflict between the day bombers and the British fighter force, a numerous German enemy against a smaller but well organized defence, and it has remained embedded in popular memory ever since.

The weekend of 14–15 September was also popularly regarded as "invasion weekend" in Britain. Troops had been put on high alert a week before, and the Air Ministry issued the "attack imminent" order to put the RAF at a state of readiness to repel invasion. The German air attacks that weekend were thus interpreted as a prelude to a more serious threat, which perhaps explains why the air victories of 15 September were seen at the time as decisive. The German attack that day consisted of two separate assaults on London, aimed at the dock areas, with around 220 bombers supported by larger numbers of fighters from Kesselring's Air Fleet 2. The German commanders also planned small subsidiary attacks on the naval base at Portland and the Spitfire factory at Southampton with aircraft of Air Fleet 3.

The first wave of bombers formed up around 11 a.m. over northern France and reached the southern coast around 11.30. This gave Park time to get at least 17 squadrons airborne, with support from neighbouring 10 and 12 Groups, a total of more than 300 fighters. The bombers and their escort were harried all the way to the target, and many German bombers jettisoned their bomb-loads early or scattered them over southern London. When they reached London,

ABOVE A Luftwaffe Dornier Do 17Z, sometimes known as the "flying pencil" due to its thin frame – an advantage as it was harder to hit than larger heavy bombers. The Dornier was used for both bombing and reconnaissance missions during the battle.

LEFT The Sector "G" Operations Room at Duxford in September 1940. The fighter squadron callsigns can be seen on the wall behind the operator, third from left. The controller is fifth from the left, and on the far right, behind the army liaison officer, are the R/T (Radio Telephone) operators in direct touch with the aircraft.

FLIGHT LIEUTENANT JOHN MUNGO-PARK (1918–1941)

John Mungo-Park was a descendant of the famous eighteenth-century explorer, Mungo Park. He joined the RAF in 1937, and was posted just after the outbreak of war to 74 Squadron based at Hornchurch in Essex. He was a flamboyant flyer and a popular commander and was one of the top-scoring British aces by the end of the battle, with at least 12 kills to his name. He commanded a squadron flight in September 1940 and took over command of the whole squadron in March 1941. During 1941, he took part in the Fighter Command operations over northern France and Belgium, known as "circuses", and was shot down and killed over the Belgian town of Adinkerke on 27 June 1941.

the bombers met a "big wing" formation flown by 12 Group from Duxford, which forced them to shed bombs wherever they could before turning tail. They were then attacked by four more fighter squadrons as they flew back in scattered formation over Kent and Sussex.

Kesselring then ordered a heavier attack to form up around 2 p.m. Fighter Command had time to refuel and reload and ample warning of the approaching force, an advantage that Kesselring could do little about since his own aircraft needed rest time after the first assault. The losses and damage of German fighter aircraft that morning meant that fewer fighters were available for the second wave, an important factor in the high losses sustained by the bombers. This time the German formation was met by more than 25 squadrons of fighters posted in the air above south-eastern England. Fierce dogfights broke out in an increasingly cloudy sky; around 185 bombers reached London and its outskirts but once again the loads were scattered at random to avoid the British fighters. One group of bombers was forced to turn back when the commanding officer of the Northolt sector, Group Captain

ABOVE RAF 66 Squadron pilots wearing their "mae wests" (life-jackets) resting in a crew-room between flights during the Battle of Britain. Souvenirs of shot-down planes can be seen on the wall above the fireplace.

BELOW A policeman stands guard as a soldier inspects a Luftwaffe Heinkel He 111K shot down in a field in Surrey on 30 August 1940.

ABOVE The view from the cockpit of a Heinkel He 111 bomber showing a Spitfire with smoke trailing after being hit in September 1940.

GENERAL ADOLF GALLAND (1912–1996)

Adolf Galland become one of the youngest commanders in the German air force when he was appointed General of Fighters in 1941, a post he held until January 1945. Fascinated from childhood by the idea of flying, he joined the still-secret air force in 1933 and almost ended his career after two serious crashes. He fought in the Condor Legion in the Spanish Civil War, and in the early stages of the Second World War became a highly decorated fighter ace, achieving 58 kills by the end of the Battle of Britain. He was shot down three times in 1941, but survived. In November 1941, he was promoted to General of Fighters and a year later was promoted to major general, when he was forced to stop flying and organize the fighter force. In 1945, after blunt arguments with Goering, he was sacked. Following the war he became an aviation consultant and businessman.

S. F. Vincent, flying unaccompanied in his Hurricane, attacked them head-on.

A large amount of damage was done by the bombers that did reach London, but it was widely dispersed, hitting the main residential areas. During the course of the day, Fighter Command lost 26 aircraft and 13 pilots. The enemy lost 36 bombers and 26 fighters destroyed, with a further 20 bombers seriously damaged. This represented a loss of approximately 25 per cent of the bomber force, a rate of attrition that no air force could sustain for more than a few days. The more serious lesson for the German side was the knowledge that the RAF was not only not close to defeat, but was stronger than ever and more tactically experienced than a month before. The following two days' poor weather prevented anything but a few limited operations, but a further daylight operation on 18 September resulted in further heavy losses and the daylight campaign petered out thereafter.

On the British side, the victories of 15 September made it more certain than ever that a German invasion could not be mounted that autumn. Park's tactics to maximize the flexibility of the defence by putting large numbers of paired squadrons in the air ready to intercept the enemy in small groups proved successful enough. The holding back of reserve squadrons to harry the returning bombers or to be thrown into a dangerous point of the battle had also proved its worth. Aircraft production in September exceeded losses by a satisfactory margin, while the number of pilots available by 15 September was the highest since the battle began in July. Battle of Britain Day saw the tide turn decisively in favour of the RAF and marked the end of the major phase of the air war by day.

RIGHT A Heinkel He 111 spotter card.

HEINKEL He.IIIK. Mk. V. (2-JUMO 2iiD)
Bomber
Span 74' 3"   Length 54' 6"   Height 13' 9"

DEFEAT OF THE DAY BOMBERS

The onset of a daylight bombing campaign on 7 September forced both sides to reconsider the way the battle was being fought. Over the following week, the attacks by day continued despite mounting German losses, while at night attacks against industrial and utility targets carried on. By the end of the month, large daylight raids had become so dangerous for the German air fleets that they were finally largely abandoned by early October and the bombing effort switched to night attacks.

Between 7 September and 5 October there were 35 major raids, 18 of them against London, the heaviest of these on 15 September. German bomber leaders insisted that they had to have a heavy fighter escort to avoid the high attrition rate suffered during the August attacks against airfields. German fighters were ordered not only to fly in front of and above the bomber stream, but also to weave in and out of the stream itself. The slow bomber speeds forced the guarding fighters to fly a zig-zag course, using up fuel needed for combat. Although the tactic generally allowed some of the bombers to reach their destination, German fighters lost the flexibility they had enjoyed in the dogfights over the British fighter stations, increasing the loss rate of fighters at a time when British numbers were steadily expanding.

Park devised a new approach to the bombing attacks. Since the German operations were consistently mounted in three waves, Park ordered 11 Group to keep six squadrons airborne to meet the first wave, a second eight squadrons to attack the next one, and the remaining squadrons to attack the third and to protect vulnerable targets. The fighters of 10 and 12 Groups were responsible for defending the airfields and facilities of 11 Group. To make sure there was time to get airborne to a sufficient height, fighter squadrons were drawn further back from the coast to give

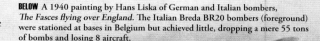

BELOW A 1940 painting by Hans Liska of German and Italian bombers, *The Fasces flying over England*. The Italian Breda BR20 bombers (foreground) were stationed at bases in Belgium but achieved little, dropping a mere 55 tons of bombs and losing 8 aircraft.

RIGHT Hermann Goering on a visit to the Channel Coast in September 1940 to receive reports about the bombing campaign. Behind him is Major General Karl Bodenschatz, the liaison officer between the air force and Hitler's supreme headquarters; to his right is Field Marshal Kesselring.

BELOW A Hurricane information card.

MARSHAL OF THE RAF SIR CHARLES PORTAL (1893–1971)

During the critical weeks of the Battle of Britain, Charles Portal was commander-in-chief of RAF Bomber Command, a post he assumed in April 1940. He began studying law in 1912, but volunteered as a dispatch rider in the Royal Engineers in 1914. A year later he joined the Royal Flying Corps and, after a distinguished wartime career, joined the infant RAF in 1919. He became director of organization in the Air Ministry from 1937–39 and was air member for personnel when he was posted to Bomber Command. An enthusiast for long-range bombing, he oversaw the first tentative attacks on German targets during the summer and autumn of 1940. In October that year, he became Chief of the Air Staff and held the post until 1945. In 1944 he was created Marshal of the Royal Air Force. After the war he played a part in the British nuclear energy programme and was later chairman of the British Aircraft Corporation from 1960–68.

HURRICANE 1 (MERLIN)
Single-Seat Fighter
Span: 40' 0" Length: 31' 5" Height: 11' 3"

them time to assemble. By relaying false height references over the radio, they were able to draw German fighters to lower levels and then to attack them from above. Hurricanes were detailed to concentrate on the bombers, Spitfires on German fighters. The new tactics immediately reduced Fighter Command losses, while the German bomber force lost 199 aircraft in the first week of attacks. In total, the German air force lost 298 aircraft in a week, a rate that could not possibly be sustained.

On 9 September, the next time a heavy attack was mounted after the big raid of the 7th, the bomber stream was diverted or turned back, and only around 90 bombers reached London. That day, 28 German aircraft were lost for the loss of 19 RAF fighters. The pattern persisted for much of September. The German side switched to diversionary fighter sweeps, or attacks with small numbers of fighter-bombers to confuse the opposition. Operations were mounted with smaller numbers of bombers and larger numbers of fighters in order to draw Fighter Command into unequal combat. Attacks continued against London, but were also carried out against aircraft production in Southampton, Bristol and elsewhere. On 30 September, three waves of attack were mounted against London with diversionary raids elsewhere, but the defences destroyed 47 German aircraft for the loss of only 20. The German commanders at last drew the obvious lesson that Fighter Command had never been defeated, and that the high bomber losses which resulted made daylight bombing too expensive to continue. From early October onwards, the day assault was ended and the night time Blitz began in earnest.

ABOVE Firemen and air raid precaution workers survey the wreckage of a German plane which crashed on to Victoria Station in London during the air battles in mid-September. Victoria was rendered inoperable on several occasions during the Blitz.

LEFT A bomb crater outside the gates of Buckingham Palace on 14 September 1940. The bomb destroyed railings but otherwise did very little damage.

BELOW A still from a newsreel film of German crew beside their crashed German bomber at West Malling, Kent in September 1940. In the first week of the bomber offensive the German air force lost 199 bombers.

EVACUATION

Long before the outbreak of war, the British government began to plan the possible evacuation of children and mothers from the main urban areas threatened by bombing. By the outbreak of war the plan was to move up to four million people from their homes. In the end only one-and-a-half million left on government schemes, with an estimated two million leaving voluntarily. Millions returned once it became clear that there would be no bombing. When the attacks on London started in September 1940, the government organized a second wave of evacuees, but only 20,500 children were moved out of London that month and a year later the figure was still only 60,000. Many families preferred to stay together and resisted evacuation plans, with the result that there was heavy loss of life among women and children during the winter of 1940–41. Evacuees were placed with foster families in less threatened rural areas and in small towns, though this did not guarantee safety. Thousands were moved to Devon, but the bombing of Exeter in April and May of 1942 resulted in the death of a number of those evacuated there during the Blitz.

BIG WINGS

One of the major controversies provoked by combat in the Battle of Britain was over the optimum size of the units Fighter Command put into the air to meet enemy aircraft. So serious did the arguments become that what was known as the "Big Wing" controversy cost Keith Park his job as commander of 11 Group and contributed to the efforts to remove Dowding from overall command.

The origins of the controversy were to be found in the sector stations of 12 Group and in particular the Duxford station, where Douglas Bader was a squadron commander. Bader and his fellow pilots were frustrated during the main part of the battle at having to guard northern airfields and installations rather than fight in the thick of the combat in "Hell's Corner" in Kent and Sussex. This was a view shared by the commander of 12 Group, Air Vice Marshal Trafford Leigh-Mallory, who resented the fact that Park, as commander of 11

Group, was in the thick of the fight. Bader developed the idea that by scrambling at least three squadrons together it would be possible to attack the enemy in real strength. These "Big Wings" would be assembled north of London at a height necessary to give the fighters the advantage, and then thrown against the bomber streams either as they attacked or, more probable given the distances involved, when they were in retreat.

BELOW LEFT The station orderly room at RAF Duxford in Cambridgeshire with RAF, WAAF and civilian clerks at work. Duxford was at the heart of the campaign for Big Wings.

BELOW The floor of a Spitfire factory in the summer of 1940. The high supply of fighter aircraft (over 1,900 during the months of the battle) ensured that Fighter Command could endure the attrition rates of battle and encouraged some commanders to think about operating fighters in much larger numbers together.

AIR VICE-MARSHAL SIR TRAFFORD LEIGH-MALLORY (1892–1944)

Commander of 12 Group during the Battle of Britain, Leigh-Mallory went on to become commander-in-chief of the Allied Expeditionary Air Force for the invasion of Normandy. He joined the Royal Flying Corps in the First World War and then stayed in the post-war RAF. In 1938, he was appointed to command 12 Group in Fighter Command and retained his command throughout the Battle of Britain. In December 1940, he succeeded Park as commander of 11 Group. In November 1942, he became commander-in-chief of Fighter Command and then of the D-Day air forces. In October 1944, he was posted to South-East Asia, but was killed in an air crash on his way to take up the post.

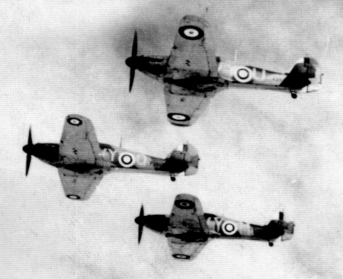

ABOVE Douglas Bader in 1940 at Duxford relaxing with crew in front of a Hurricane. Bader was the principal spokesman for the idea of "Big Wings".

MAIN PICTURE Hurricanes of 12 Group's 85 Squadron from Church Fenton in north Yorkshire in flight on 23 October 1940. The larger formations were supposed to be able to inflict heavier damage on attacking aircraft but the evidence remained ambiguous.

ABOVE A group of Italian airmen in North Africa in discussion with General Italo Balbo in 1940. "Big Wings" were also known by the nickname "Balbos" because of the Italian commander's reputation for leading large air units.

During the attacks on the fighter stations of 11 Group, Park had many times asked Leigh-Mallory to provide one or two squadrons to protect the more northerly airfields. In a number of cases the 12 Group squadrons had failed to appear. Instead they were assembled in large wings of up to five squadrons, which took a considerable time, and sent out to engage enemy formations in 11 Group's airspace. On 17 September, Leigh-Mallory submitted an exaggerated report to the Air Ministry claiming that in five such "Big Wing" operations, 163 enemy aircraft had been accounted for, for the loss of only 14 fighters and six pilots. He found allies in the Air Ministry, particularly Sholto Douglas, the assistant chief of staff. Harold Balfour, Under Secretary of State for Air, provided political support. During the last part of September and early October, strong criticism emerged of Park's tactics which he had little time to contest.

Park had been compelled by the scattered nature of German objectives and the size of his force to operate squadrons in pairs. The difficulty of ensuring rendezvous meant that squadrons on many occasions intercepted the enemy on their own. But using his aircraft in small groups meant that every element of a German attack could be opposed, while allowing some reserve squadrons to be held back to throw into the most dangerous parts of the battle. This system had worked well with the help of aircraft from 10 Group, which had protected sector stations. 12 Group, on the other hand, had been reluctant to supply help and on occasion arrived only after a fighter station had already been bombed. Park's complaints about Leigh-Mallory prompted a high-level conference at the Air Ministry on 17 October at which all the issues were thrashed out. Leigh-Mallory defied protocol by bringing with him

Douglas Bader, a junior officer, and at the meeting Bader's claims were used by Park's critics as the basis for a comprehensive rejection of his tactics. There followed a month's campaign in the Air Ministry to champion the idea of "Big Wings" and to remove Park from command.

During late September and October, Leigh-Mallory failed to co-operate effectively with 11 Group. For almost a month the "Big Wings" regularly sent south from 12 Group's sector stations failed to engage the enemy once. A classic example was the German attack on 29 October when Park called for 12 Group wings to intercept raids in the morning and late afternoon. On both occasions the wings took so long to assemble that they failed to intercept while Park had 17 squadrons airborne at the critical moment. None of these failings could dissuade those hostile to Park (and increasingly hostile to Dowding as well) from the idea that using fighters in large numbers represented a tactical advantage. In November, Park was notified that he was to be relieved as commander of 11 Group, to be replaced by Leigh-Mallory. Dowding had already been informed that he was to be stood down from the RAF and his replacement would be Sholto Douglas, leading spokesman of the campaign against Park.

During 1941 Douglas and Leigh-Mallory had the opportunity to use "Big Wings" in regular fighter assaults on northern Europe generally known as "Circuses". The outcome was an exceptionally high level of casualties, with a 44 per cent rate of loss over the two years of the campaign. The results demonstrated that aggressively large numbers of fighters did not necessarily represent a tactical advantage, as Park had argued all along.

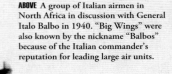

WING COMMANDER DOUGLAS BADER (1910–1982)

The son of a soldier, Douglas Bader was one of a generation of young university graduates attracted into a career in flying. He joined the RAF in 1928 but was invalided out after crashing his plane late in 1931 and losing both legs. He proved able to fly with artificial limbs, and on the outbreak of war in 1939 managed to persuade the RAF to reinstate him. He became a squadron leader in June 1940 and was posted to Duxford air base in command of a squadron of Hurricanes during the Battle of Britain. He shot down his first German aircraft of the battle in July. He was an inspirational commander and a fine pilot, recording at least 22 kills. In August 1941, he was shot down in a raid over France. He tried to escape from German POW camps on a number of occasions and was eventually incarcerated in Colditz Castle from where he was liberated in April 1945.

SEALION POSTPONED

For Hitler and the German High Command, the whole purpose of the Battle of Britain had been to destroy the RAF as an effective defensive force in order to open the way for a rapid invasion of southern England in September. Operation Sealion envisaged landing up to nine divisions of the 9th and 16th German armies on a front from Deal in Kent to Rottingdean in Sussex. Rapid reinforcements, supported by air forces, would then aim first for a line from Gravesend to Portsmouth, then a second line from the Essex coast to the Severn Estuary, including the capture of London. The invasion date had been fixed provisionally for 15 September.

On 30 August, the date was switched to 20 September to allow the navy to complete its build-up. Barges, motor boats, tugs and large transport craft were assembled in the ports along the coastline facing southern England, a total of 3,494 vessels of all kinds. These were subjected to persistent though not heavy attacks by Bomber Command from July onwards, but fewer than 10 per cent of the boats were destroyed or damaged. The issues that mattered for German planners

were the weather, which was expected to deteriorate steadily over the autumn weeks, and the evident failure to eliminate the RAF, either Fighter or Bomber Command. The Royal Navy also constituted a serious obstacle to any possible landing. In conferences in the first two weeks of September, the navy commander-in-chief, Grand Admiral Raeder, told Hitler that the conditions for a successful landing had not been met and recommended an indirect strategy of blockade. On 14 September, Hitler assembled his commanders for a final conference on "the England problem". He told them that preparations were complete but the risk from the air was still too great. He postponed a final decision until 17 September, by which time the air battles two days previously had demonstrated decisively that the German air force had failed to gain air superiority.

On 17 September Hitler decided to postpone Sealion indefinitely, though he did not rule out an operation in October. A directive two days later ordered preparations to be scaled down and barges and transports began to leave the Channel ports. On 12 October, Hitler

CODEWORD CROMWELL

In the summer of 1940, British forces prepared for possible invasion. The preparations included two signals to be sent out to forces in the event of a probable German landing. The first was for eight hours' notice, the second, activated by the codeword CROMWELL, was for immediate action. On 7 September, the information suggested an imminent invasion and in the evening of that day the signal CROMWELL was sent to all units in eastern and southern England. The RAF had a three-level warning with number one, "attack imminent", as the most severe. On 7 September, that warning was also sent out to all air squadrons. The warnings caused some panic and sightings were reported of German parachutists and German boats, but all proved groundless. Not until 25 October did the RAF release the signal to units that invasion was improbable, by which stage it was evident that German forces were not going to come that autumn.

ABOVE RIGHT The German foreign minister Joachim von Ribbentrop greets his Soviet counterpart, Vyacheslav Molotov, as he arrives at a station in Berlin on 12 November 1940. Discussions proved fruitless and Hitler decided to attack the Soviet Union the following spring.

LEFT Members of the Home Guard training with a Lewis gun in 1940 at a Weapons Training School. German commanders had orders to treat them like partisans and shoot them.

BELOW Two soldiers stand guard on a beach with a barbed wire barricade in southern England on 2 September 1940. Five days later the alert was given for imminent invasion.

THE GERMAN BLOCKADE

One of the central features of German strategy during 1940 was to find ways of blockading British trade and undermining British war-willingness and the British war economy. Throughout the Battle of Britain and beyond, German aircraft and submarines attacked British vessels around the coast, in port or in the western approaches to the British Isles. During 1940, over 1,000 ships were sunk, totalling four million tons, one-quarter of the British merchant fleet. By 1941, British imports were down to 38 per cent of the level of 1938. The food crisis was met by rationing and large scale propaganda for turning gardens and parks into allotments for growing food. By the end of the war, there were 1.7 million allotments, producing enough food to secure reasonable rations and to reduce food imports by half.

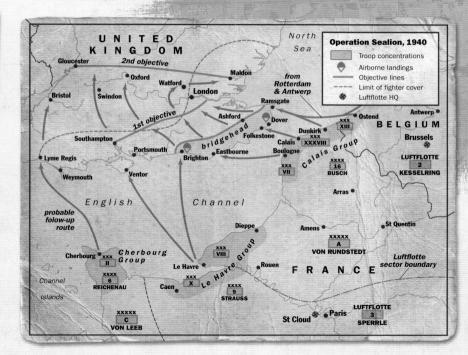

USE SPADES NOT SHIPS

GROW YOUR OWN FOOD
AND SUPPLY YOUR OWN COOKHOUSE

announced that any landing in 1940 was ruled out but that the impression of possible invasion should be maintained so as to put continuous pressure on British resolve. German air forces were now to bear the responsibility for trying to force Britain out of the war by a sustained campaign of night-bombing against major ports and cities. On the British side, the German decision was difficult to interpret. Photo reconnaissance showed that the number of barges clearly visible had declined from 1,004 on 18 September to only 448 in the last week of October, but many more could be seen waiting on canals not much further inland. The state of readiness in Britain was only relaxed towards the end of October, but there remained strong fears that the German threat would be renewed in the spring and British planning had to be based on that possibility.

In fact Hitler had now turned to face a different enemy. Already in July, he had hinted at a possible swift blow against the Soviet Union in the early summer of 1941. During September, planning

went ahead for the invasion, organized by General Friedrich Paulus (later defeated at Stalingrad). From 12–13 November 1940, the Soviet foreign minister, Vyacheslav Molotov, visited Berlin to try to negotiate new agreements over spheres of influence in Eastern Europe. The discussions, interrupted by an RAF raid which forced Molotov and von Ribbentrop to shelter in an underground bunker, showed Hitler that the Soviet appetite for further gains was growing and he finally approved preparations for an invasion. On 18 December, he signed Directive 21 "Operation Barbarossa" for an annihilating assault on the Soviet Union in May 1941. He planned to settle with Britain again after the defeat of the Red Army and the acquisition of vast Russian resources.

ABOVE A map of the planned German assault on southern England in autumn 1940, to be mounted from three separate areas on the southern Channel coast. The operation was designed to secure a bridgehead in Kent and Sussex, then to seize London and finally to reach a line from the Bristol Channel to East Anglia. By this time it was hoped that the British government would sue for peace.

BELOW Bombs explode during an attack by RAF Bomber Command on barges at Boulogne destined to take part in the German invasion. Almost 1,000 tons of bombs were dropped on the Channel ports in September 1940 though only around 10 per cent of German shipping was destroyed.

BELOW German troops rehearsing the invasion of southern England in the late summer of 1940. In the background is a ship converted to a transport and landing role. German forces trained hard for the amphibious operation but there was little experience on which to draw.

53

The German change to night bombing in October 1940 transformed the nature of the air battle as Fighter Command had to switch some of its effort to contesting the new campaign. By 3 November, there were 11 night-fighter squadrons and one night-fighter flight available, composed mainly of Blenheim, Beaufighter and Defiant aircraft, but with 3.5 Hurricane squadrons as well. The night fighters could achieve little without effective radar equipment and interception of enemy aircraft was largely accidental. It was the relative failure of the night-fighter campaign that contributed to the decision to remove Dowding in November. During October 1940, the German air force lost a further 365 aircraft, but more than half the losses sustained by German bombers from October onwards were the result of accidents caused by poor weather, ice and the difficulties of night-time navigation.

The day battle continued at a reduced level of intensity and with changed tactics. German air fleets sent over a large number of smaller raids by day using aircraft converted to a fighter-bomber role, usually protected by an extensive fighter screen. The purpose of these small hit-and-run attacks was to keep up pressure on the British civilian population round the clock, and to lure Fighter Command into fighter-to-fighter contests in which it was hoped that a high rate of attrition could be exacted from a force still thought to be close to

ABOVE A crowd watches a newsreel on the RAF carried by a mobile cinema in October 1940. The films were designed to help raise money for the air effort, and thousands of pounds were given to help communities buy and donate their own Spitfire.

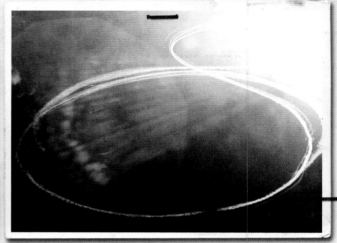

BELOW German Dornier Do17 bombers over southern England during the Battle of Britain. These and other bomber aircraft engaged in small hit-and-run raids during October and November.

ABOVE As the days grew colder in the late autumn, aircraft left spectacular vapour trails in the sky. Here the Spitfires of 41 Squadron leave their mark over Hornchurch, Essex in October 1940.

AIR CHIEF MARSHAL SHOLTO DOUGLAS (1893–1969)

Dowding's successor as commander-in-chief of Fighter Command was Sholto Douglas, a career airman with a reputation for speaking his mind. He joined the Royal Flying Corps in 1914 and had a distinguished career as commander of 84 Squadron. He worked briefly as a commercial pilot before rejoining the RAF in 1920. In 1938, he became assistant chief of staff and in November 1940 succeeded Dowding as head of Fighter Command. In 1942 he was sent to be RAF Commander-in-Chief Middle East and in 1944 took charge of Coastal Command. After the war, he became military governor of the British zone of occupation in Germany from 1946–47. He retired in 1948 and became chairman of British European Airways from 1949 to 1964.

"NEVER WAS SO MUCH OWED BY SO MANY TO SO FEW" *THE PRIME MINISTER*

MEMORABILIA

ITEM 16: A letter dated 1 August from Sholto Douglas at the Air Ministry to Dowding describing the different states of alert in preparation for a German invasion. On 27 August the order of the alerts was reversed, with 1 becoming "attack imminent". The change caused considerable confusion.

ITEM 17: Cipher message dated 7 September showing "invasion imminent" for the following day.

ITEM 18: On 24 September 1940 Squadron Leader Harold Bird-Wilson was shot down by the German ace Adolf Galland over the Thames. This is a photograph of the Hurricane he was flying.

ITEM 19: Telegram sent by Squadron Leader Harold Bird-Wilson to his family on 24 September 1940 reporting that he was still alive.

ITEM 20: Letter sent to Bird-Wilson in hospital giving him news of the air battle.

TELEPHONE:

ABBEY 3411.

Extn. ....

Any communications on the
subject of this letter should
be addressed to :—

THE
UNDER SECRETARY
OF STATE,
and the following number
quoted :—

S. 5723/D.C.A.S.

AIR MINISTRY,

LONDON, S.W.1.

1st August, 1940.

SECRET.

Sir,

<u>ANTI-INVASION PLANS — STANDARDISATION OF
STATES OF READINESS.</u>

     I am directed to inform you that the question of
standardising some system - preferably common to the three
Services - for ensuring a similar degree of readiness in which
the armed forces are required to be held against any impending
invasion threat, has been under consideration.

2.   Before carrying this project to the stage of inter-
departmental discussion it is desired to obtain the opinion of
Air Officers Commanding-in-Chief upon the utility and application of this proposal.

3.   It is proposed that there should be three states of
readiness imposed by higher authority:-

    <u>Readiness No. 1</u> - When attack is regarded as improbable
      within the following three days, although an invasion
      threat is believed to exist.

    <u>Readiness No. 2</u> - When attack is regarded as probable
      within the following three days.

    <u>Readiness No. 3</u> - When attack is regarded as imminent and
      likely to occur within the next 12 hours.

4.   I am to say that under this scheme it would be
required that instructions should be issued throughout operational commands and Flying Training Command, defining the fore-
going states of readiness, laying down the outline of any
action to be taken at the Formation Headquarters issuing the
instructions, and requiring subordinate Formation Headquarters
and units to maintain corresponding tabulations for each state
of readiness. It is thought that such a tabulation of the
preparatory duties to be performed by various branches of
Command Staffs and at subordinate formations would ensure that
detail matters of preparation would not, in the stress of
circumstances, be overlooked.

5.   It is appreciated that the nature of the preparations
to be undertaken must depend largely upon the geographical
location of the expected attack, and whether by air-borne or
sea-borne forces. Certain precautionary measures which would

/be

The Air Officer Commanding-in-Chief,
    Headquarters, Fighter Command,
      Royal Air Force,
        Stanmore,
          Middlesex.

be taken in an area believed to have been selected for invasion
would differ from those in an area believed to be immune.
To meet this requirement it is suggested that the readiness
warning order should be followed by any definition possible at
the time to indicate the most probable regions for enemy attack,
e.g., 'Eastern', 'Ireland' or 'Shetlands'. Any closer definition might be added.

6.   I am to request that you will forward your comments on
these proposals by 8th August.   I am also to ask that consideration may be given, at your Headquarters and at subordinate formations, to the actual tabulation of readiness action to be taken
for the three degrees of readiness described above in relation to
specific natures and locations of enemy attack.   By this means it
is hoped to be in a position to put the scheme into effect as soon
as agreement is reached, and by its application to avoid delay and
confusion during a period when disorganisation would be likely to
occur as the result of heavy and sustained enemy air attack.   A
copy of Readiness Tables and Instructions issued by Headquarters,
British Air Forces in France, is enclosed herewith for reference
and to clarify the nature of the organisation proposed.

                    I am,
                        Sir,
                    Your obedient Servant,

                         W.S. Douglas

                    Air Vice-Marshal.
                Deputy Chief of the Air Staff.

R.A.F. Form 683.

Wt. 43513-4/4141-2   900 M (2 sorts) 3/40............51/6255

SECRET.
CYPHER MESSAGE.

Immediate

To— AOC in C Bomber Fighter Coastal AOC Flying Training Command AOC 22 group AOC RAF in Ireland RNAB HQ	Date	7/9	
		Receipt	Despatch
	Time of	2214	
From— Air Min Home forces	System		

Serial No. 791

X 3 22   7/9 ⊙

Until 000·1 hours Sept 8 invasion alert no. 2 continues ⊙ Invasion alert no. 1 is introduced at 0001 hrs Sept 8 ⊙ Probable area is SOUTHWOLD to BEACHY HEAD

Received 2250
7 Sept
[signature]

= 1916

[signature]

CYPHER MESSAGE

ACTION COPIED

INFORMATION COPIED

"   "   "

"   "   "

DATE

1

"B" FLIGHT NO 17 SQUADRON

HURRICANE P 3878 (UNTIL DESTROYED) 24 SEPT 1940   ITEM 18

24th September 1940

Charges to pay

_____s._____d.

RECEIVED

PM 3 18

_____m

POST OFFICE TELEGRAM

CONFIRMATION ALDERSHOT 24 SEP 40 HANTS.

No. _____

OFFICE STAMP

Prefix. Time handed in. Office of Origin and Service Instructions. Words. 3-23 m

From _____ 96 196 2-29 CHATHAM 13 To _____ RD131

PRIORITY

-PRIORITY- WALLIS RUNFOLD 131 =

Wayside Blighton Lane Seale

IN NAVAL HOSPITAL CHATHAM EVERYTHING OK. WRITING SOON =

BIRDY +

P.T.O.

131 +

For free repetition of doubtful words telephone "TELEGRAMS ENQUIRY" or call, with this form at office of delivery. Other enquiries should be accompanied by this form and, if possible, the envelope.

B or C

(67256) WT T3204/6412 75000 PADS 9/39 MANIFOLDIA 51/4734

25/8/99
Copy taken by Philip Craig of
Brook Lapping re BBC programme.
re Battle of Britain. "Finest Hour"
to be shown Nov/Dec 1999.

& if there is anything
else you want just
let us know & we will
send it along.

Winsler, who as
you know was hit at
the same time as you,
is back about the men
& will be going on some
leave in a day or two.

We saw the best
sight ever yesterday.
30 the 110s milling
around over London
— the usual odd
Hurricanes chewing
bits off them — nearly

ROYAL AIR FORCE,
DEBDEN,
SAFFRON WALDEN,
ESSEX.
TELEPHONES, SAFFRON WALDEN 351.

Saturday —

Dear Birdie,

Just a note to say
how bloody glad we all
were to see you get
out of that Hurricane &
hit the silk — also
to see the boat get to
you so promptly.

Hope you didn't find
the swim too cold.

Baddeas is bringing
your kit down to you

all our chaps had a
squirt at them & then
two complete squadrons
of Hurricanes arrived
& slashed them followed
by the Duxford Balbo
of three squadrons —
never laughed so much
for a long time — we
only saw three out of the
whole bunch get across
the coast.

Sgt Griffiths got three
that day —. two —two
110s & one 109.

Hope you find
your hospital a good

4

then — Esn - & partly shopping
moves, & that sort of thing

Best wishes from all

Yours

G. S. Abel

extinction. The fighter-bomber attacks did not achieve a great deal, but RAF pilots found themselves at a disadvantage against large groups of high-flying German fighters, which had better facilities and more effective engines for combat over 6,000 metres (20,000 feet). Both forces by this stage were strained by the weeks of intensive combat, but many pilots now had substantial combat experience and the dogfights in October and November 1940 pitted rival aces against each other.

To cope with the change in the pattern of German attack, Park ordered a new tactical approach. Standing patrols of high-flying Spitfires were sent up to give advance warning of approaching German fighters. Once the enemy had been identified, other squadrons patrolling at lower altitudes could be brought swiftly to the height necessary to engage the intruders. This did not solve the problem of the technical superiority of the Messerschmitt Me 109 at altitude, and 165 Spitfires and Hurricanes were shot down during October. Many of the contests were a result of Fighter Command rising to the German challenge. In reality, the fighter attacks represented little real risk to the British war effort and might have been absorbed at a much lower level of effort than Fighter Command eventually mounted. During October, 253 raids were mounted and

in November a further 235. This was a heavy burden for both tired forces to sustain and by late November the campaign petered out. Smaller German raids persisted over the following three years of war until the arrival of the vengeance weapons – the V1 pilotless bomb and the V2 rocket – in the summer and autumn of 1944.

The real crisis confronted by Fighter Command in the autumn of 1940 was not the daylight threat but the failure to stem the tide of German night bombing. Despite high levels of attrition exacted from the German air forces from August onwards, it was difficult to prevent much of the bombing from taking place. It was this that contributed to the growing unease felt in the Air Ministry and in political circles about whether or not Dowding was adequate to the job of defending Britain. Though admired by Churchill, Dowding could do little about the whispering campaign. On 13 November, he was informed that he had been chosen to head a top-level mission to the United States; four days later he was told to give up his command immediately. It was found that his designated successor, Sholto Douglas, could not take over until 25 November so for another week Dowding agreed to stay in command. He sent a farewell message addressed to his "Fighter Boys" in which he repeated Churchill's stirring phrase about the few and the many as the only fitting tribute.

MAJOR HELMUT WICK (1915–1940)

One of the leading German air aces, Helmut Wick joined the German air force in 1935. He was rapidly promoted and in 1939 served in the squadron commanded by Werner Mölders. On the outbreak of war, he was flying with the "Richthofen" fighter wing and shot down his first aircraft on 22 November 1939. He enjoyed continued success, and was made a captain in September 1940 and commander of a fighter group. In October, he was made the youngest major in the air force and took over full command of the "Richthofen" unit. On the morning of 28 November, Wick made his 56th kill, making him the highest-scoring German ace, but a few minutes later he was shot down by a Spitfire near the Isle of Wight. Neither his aircraft nor his body were subsequently found.

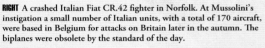
RIGHT A crashed Italian Fiat CR.42 fighter in Norfolk. At Mussolini's instigation a small number of Italian units, with a total of 170 aircraft, were based in Belgium for attacks on Britain later in the autumn. The biplanes were obsolete by the standard of the day.

BELOW The altar of St Paul's Cathedral surrounded by debris from the roof after a bomb attack in October 1940. The survival of the cathedral later came to symbolize British defiance of Hitler.

BELOW The wreckage of a Messerschmitt Me 109 after it had crashed into a haystack on a farm on the outskirts of London on 9 October 1940. The air battles that month took a high toll of both sides for little strategic advantage.

THE NIGHT BLITZ

◎ SEPTEMBER 1940–MAY 1941

The decision by the German high command to embark on a strategy of independent bombing from September onwards rested on an act of faith that bombing might – as so many had predicted between the wars – force an enemy to surrender without a conventional ground invasion. It is not clear that Hitler had much confidence in the outcome and he insisted in September that the air force should not engage in terror attacks for their own sake. Most of the air force commanders accepted the view that bombing people achieved little, except dead people, while attacks against ports, shipping, stocks and communications might disrupt the British war effort sufficiently to produce the secondary effect of demoralization.

Nevertheless, there were politicians and commanders in Germany who hoped that the campaign would turn into a campaign against morale. The so-called "England Committee" in von Ribbentrop's Foreign Office favoured a short terror campaign in autumn 1940 to force Britain out of the war. Joseph Goebbels, the Minister for

Propaganda, authorized German newspapers to publicize the bombing to help boost German opinion, but he also believed the exaggerated interwar predictions about how unendurable bombing was. In November, he wrote in his diary, "When will Churchill capitulate?" On 5 December, he recorded the extensive bombing of the port of Southampton: "the city is one single ruin … and so it must go on until England is on her knees, begging for peace". The German air force chief of staff, Hans Jeschonnek was also among those who imagined a terror campaign might produce real results, but he had to accept Hitler's restraining hand and the system of targeting continued to be based on economic and military priorities.

The night Blitz was concentrated on London, which experienced 57 consecutive days of bombing from 7 September to 2 November, and then intermittent and heavy bombing thereafter until 10 May. 18,000 tons of heavy explosive and incendiary bombs were dropped on London compared with 1,228 tons dropped on Plymouth, one

THE ANDERSON SHELTER

The sturdy metal garden shelter designed in 1938 by William Paterson and Oscar Kerrison was named after Sir John Anderson, the government minister responsible for preparing air-raid precautions. The shelter was made of 14 corrugated steel panels, with a curved roof section which was supposed to be covered by at least 0.4 metres (15 inches) of soil. They were issued free to householders with an income of less than £250 a year and there was also help with installation costs. Some 3.6 million shelters were distributed between February 1939 and the end of the war. They held up to six people and could contain bunks and other small items of furniture. The shelters were not able to withstand a direct hit and many became waterlogged. Those shelters deemed by the authorities to be unsuitable because of water either had a concrete floor laid down or were removed altogether, forcing the household to use local public shelters. At the end of the war, they were supposed to be returned to the authorities for scrap, but could be kept on payment of a small fee.

IT'S DANGEROUS TO FLAG A BUS WITH YOUR TORCH

ABOVE One of many posters telling people how to behave in the blackout. When blackout regulations were introduced on 1 September 1939, few people could have imagined that they would become a permanent feature of the next five years.

RIGHT Air raid precaution workers in the ruins of a London street following a raid on 7 October 1940. Two-thirds of all bombs in the Blitz fell on London where an army of volunteers helped to provide emergency housing, food and medical assistance.

The reactions of the British public to the effects of bombing were mixed. There were mass flights from bombed towns into the surrounding countryside. Crime levels temporarily increased with new opportunities for looting. In London there was some political agitation in the East End about poor levels of protection and against the capital's Jewish population, which was accused of seeking shelter first. But in general, the reaction was one of resignation and determination. Millions of ordinary civilians found the courage and capacity to organize an army of volunteers for air-raid precautions, auxiliary fire services, nursing and first aid and the rehabilitation of bomb victims. These were civilians who saw themselves as soldiers of the home front and in 1942, to acknowledge their sacrifice, the Ministry of Information published the booklet "Frontline 1940–1941", designed to make it clear that total war as waged by the German armed forces compelled everyone on the home front to become a kind of civilian-soldier whether they liked it or not.

of the most heavily destroyed targets after London. Heavy attacks were made on Belfast, Glasgow, Bristol, Birmingham, Liverpool, Manchester, Sheffield and Hull. The attack on Coventry on the night of 14–15 November 1940 attracted more attention than almost any other, partly because of the high number of deaths in a single raid, an estimated 554. In total, around 11,800 tons of bombs were dropped on targets outside London, and these accounted for around 50 per cent of the casualties. This was partly due to the fact that areas outside London were generally less well protected by anti-aircraft guns and had a lower level of civil defence preparation (and fewer shelters). The level of casualties was high in Britain because bomb attacks were directed against crowded working-class districts around port facilities, and because air-raid precautions were activated in an uneven pattern across the country. Over the course of the campaign, the German air force also tried to work out more destructive forms of attack using a higher ratio of incendiary bombs.

ABOVE Londoners listening to a concert in the London Underground station at Aldwych where they had sought shelter on 21 October 1940. This station was among the first converted to provide shelter in September 1940. It was closed to trains and the tracks covered in concrete.

RIGHT A Junkers Ju 88 spotter card.

JUNKERS Ju.88 A-I (JUMO 2II)
Long Range Bomber
Span: 59' 0" Length: 46' 6" Height: 15' 0"

MASS OBSERVATION

Founded in 1937 by the anthropologist Tom Harrisson, the poet Charles Madge and the documentary film-maker Humphrey Jennings, Mass Observation (MO) was intended to record the feelings and outlook of ordinary British people. Thousands of volunteers were recruited who kept a record of conversations they heard and behaviour they observed. These records were used to help compile consolidated reports on aspects of everyday life. In September 1939, Harrisson took over the running of the whole MO organization. From September 1940 until the middle of 1941, a detailed record was kept of attitudes to the Blitz. Harrisson himself toured round the blitzed cities to form his own impressions. He eventually went on to write *Living Through the Blitz*, published shortly after his death in 1976. There was some official hostility to MO, but the organization shared some of its findings with the Ministry of Information as the war went on. Mass Observation left an invaluable record of the impact on ordinary people of a campaign of sustained bombing.

BELOW Earl Street in Coventry following the disastrous raid of 14–15 November 1940. Much of the city centre, including the cathedral, was destroyed. The government chose to release the details to the press, the first time a city had actually been named in newspaper reports.

THE COSTS OF BATTLE

THE GUINEA PIG CLUB

The Guinea Pig Club was founded by the patients of the remarkable New Zealand plastic surgeon Archibald McIndoe. Its members were aircrew who had required extensive surgery as a result of severe burns. McIndoe set up a unit for plastic and jaw surgery at the Queen Victoria Hospital in East Grinstead, Surrey in 1939. He believed that patients needed general care as well as surgery, and the club ensured that those who had gone through a difficult hospitalization would be able to share their experience with others. The Guinea Pig Club was founded in the summer of 1941 and initially had 39 members from among the patients McIndoe had treated since the air battles of 1940, as well as the hospital staff. There were eventually 649 members and they produced a magazine called *Guinea Pig* which appeared until 2003. McIndoe died in 1960 at the age of 59, and is the only civilian interred in the RAF church of St Clement Danes on the Strand in London.

The costs of the Battle of Britain are difficult to assess with complete accuracy. The number of Fighter Command crew lost was once calculated at 449, but recent estimates put it at 544. Total German aircrew losses were much higher because the bombers typically carried a crew of four or five. In addition, 967 German aircrew prisoners were identified from the period between 1 July and 31 October 1940, while only 638 of the many maimed and burnt bodies that crashed on English territory could be positively identified. Hundreds of airmen on both sides were also injured, seriously wounded or simply exhausted by the long period of intense action.

The number of dead was tiny in comparison with any ground action, or even the sinking of a major ship, and small in relation to the significance of the battle itself. In this sense Churchill's notion of "the Few" can be understood more readily. There were also casualties among ground crew and support staff, both male and female, and a considerable amount of serious damage to a handful of RAF stations. The losses of pilots and aircraft were generally made good, so that by the end of the battle Fighter Command had more aircraft and pilots on hand than at its start. By contrast, German losses caused a temporary decline in numbers so that by the end of the year the German fighter force was reduced by around 30 per cent and the bomber force by a quarter. The nature of air conflict, in which trained men and new aircraft can be prepared far from the battlefield and thrown into the conflict at any point, meant that although the RAF succeeded in preventing German air superiority over southern Britain, neither force could effectively be destroyed by the other.

ABOVE Rescue workers pull a victim from the rubble trapped in a bomb-damaged building following heavy air raids on London during the Blitz.

BELOW St Paul's Cathedral rises above the ruins that have surrounded it during five years of war. An elaborate plan was drawn up for the rebuilding of the City of London but reconstruction lasted for years, partly because of legal arguments over ownership of the ruins.

The cost of the battle was borne more heavily by the civilian population, which was subjected to regular bombing from July 1940 onwards and then to a heavy assault from early September. During the period up to the middle of 1941, over 43,000 people were killed, almost half of them in London and the surrounding area. A larger number sustained major or minor injuries, but the exact figure is uncertain. The high rate of expected psychiatric casualties from bombing did not materialize; the number of people admitted for treatment actually declined during the period of the bombing. In addition to the deaths and injuries, over one million housing units were destroyed or seriously damaged. This required evacuation to safer areas or the billeting of bombed-out families on households where there had not been damage. Schools were destroyed and many young Londoners missed long periods of schooling at the height of the bombing emergency.

The economic and military damage caused by the bombing was a good deal lighter than the German side had hoped. Aircraft production was held up for a few weeks after attacks on the Supermarine factories at Southampton and the Spitfire factory at Castle Bromwich in Birmingham. But the assault on British stores of food and other materials in the major ports did not prove too disruptive. In five months of bombing a total of around 70,000 tons of food stocks were destroyed but only 0.5 per cent of Britain's stored oil reserves were lost. Interruption to utilities and services could be restored quickly and the overall impact on the productivity of the British war economy was small in relation to the cost to the Germans of their assault.

The battle did have the effect of galvanizing the British public in ways which defeat in France or Norway had not. Some 600,000 volunteers worked in the civil defence forces in addition to the tens of thousands who worked in other volunteer capacities for the home front. The period of the Battle of Britain and the Blitz was the point at which most British people came to understand the dimensions of total war fought not only between armed forces but against the civilian population as well. German hopes that British morale on the home front might crack in 1940 proved misplaced, but the cost in suffering, loss and dislocation caused by the campaign was real enough.

CASUALTIES

AIRCRAFT LOSSES JULY–OCTOBER 1940

German air force 1,887
RAF Fighter Command 1,023
RAF Bomber Command 376
RAF Coastal Command 148

AIRCREW LOSSES JULY–OCTOBER 1940

German air force 2,698
RAF Fighter Command 544
(5 Belgians, 7 Czechs, 29 Poles, 3 Canadians, 3 New Zealanders, 2 Americans)

"NEVER WAS SO MUCH OWED BY SO MANY TO SO FEW"
THE PRIME MINISTER

BELOW A scrapyard of German aircraft from the air battles over England. The materials were recycled to help with war production while German equipment was carefully examined to see what lessons the British could learn.

RIGHT One of the most famous British posters of the war illustrates the heroic status enjoyed by Britain's fighter pilots after the Battle of Britain. Pilots joked that Churchill's phrase referred to their mess bills.

REMEMBERING THE BATTLE

Memory of the Battle of Britain was soon given official status when the Air Ministry produced a small 32-page booklet on the battle in March 1941. The Ministry sold over one million copies in Britain, and more in America and the Empire. The dates for the battle were set as 8 August to 31 October, but by the time the official histories were written the dates generally accepted were 10 July to 31 October, to incorporate the early raids and air battles. The major operations on 15 September were chosen to mark Battle of Britain Day and the first celebration took place in 1945, shortly after the end of the war with Japan, with a fly-past in London and a special memorial service in Westminster Abbey.

The abbey was also the home of the Battle of Britain Chapel, dedicated on 10 July 1947 to indicate clearly the day the battle was now thought to have begun. Its centrepiece was a stained glass window

BELOW The Battle of Britain Memorial Day ceremony at Capel-le-Ferne in Kent in July 2009. Veterans of the battle lay wreaths at the statue of a fighter pilot, which dominates the memorial itself.

and a roll of honour was also presented with 1,495 names of pilots and aircrew from Fighter, Bomber and Coastal Command, and the Fleet Air Arm. The chapel became the site for an annual Battle of Britain service. In the 1950s, the Air Ministry searched for other ways of commemorating the battle and in 1957 a Battle of Britain Historic Flight was set up, including three Spitfires and a Hurricane. It was renamed the Battle of Britain Memorial Flight in 1969 and its aircraft appeared regularly at air shows around the country. To mark the sixtieth anniversary of the battle in 2000, the Imperial War Museum annual air show at Duxford (the former Fighter Command station) brought together all the remaining UK-based Spitfires still capable of flying for a final historic fly-past.

The veterans of the battle also began to meet regularly and in 1958 a formal organization, the Battle of Britain Fighter Association, was formed, whose first president was Hugh Dowding. On his death in 1970, he was succeeded by Keith Park.

BATTLE OF BRITAIN

In 1969, one of the most famous of all British war films was released, *Battle of Britain*. Produced by Harry Saltzman and S. Benjamin Fisz, the film's cast was a roll call of famous British actors and actresses, including Laurence Olivier as Hugh Dowding and Trevor Howard as Keith Park.

Unusually, the German parts were played by native Germans and their conversation subtitled. Over 100 aircraft were used in making the film, including a dozen airworthy Spitfires and three Hurricanes still capable of flying. The German aircraft were represented by Spanish versions of the Heinkel He111 bombers and Messerschmitt Me109 fighters which had served in the Spanish air force. They were powered by British Merlin engines. Filming took place at four surviving Fighter Command stations, including Duxford, where a hangar was blown up for the film. Poor weather hampered production and shots of clear blue skies were filmed in Spain.

"Battle of Britain"

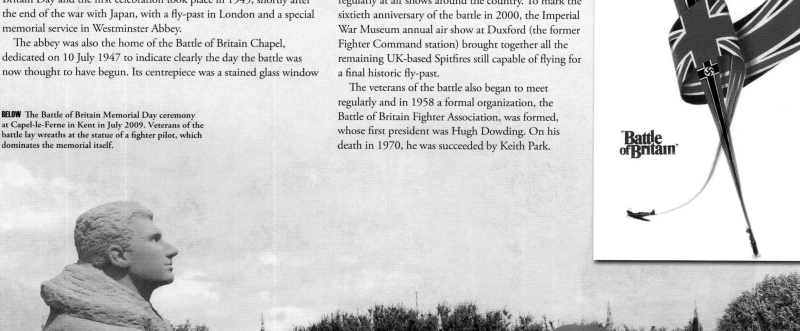

RIGHT The Battle of Britain Memorial Flight, first set up in the 1950s, which now consists of a Spitfire and Hurricane fighter and an Avro Lancaster bomber. The flight is used for formal fly-pasts and also as a spectacle at the many air shows where the Battle of Britain is still commemorated.

BELOW To the south of Croydon airport on the Purley Way stands a Battle of Britain monument erected in 1991. The 23 foot obelisk is topped by a bronze eagle and bears on it the names of those who died in the battle.

ABOVE Douglas Bader (left), Arthur Clouston (centre), and Keith Park (right) at a ceremony in February 1948 to name a locomotive "Fighter Pilot".

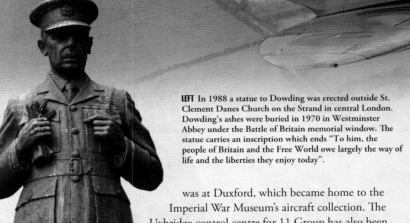

LEFT In 1988 a statue to Dowding was erected outside St. Clement Danes Church on the Strand in central London. Dowding's ashes were buried in 1970 in Westminster Abbey under the Battle of Britain memorial window. The statue carries an inscription which ends "To him, the people of Britain and the Free World owe largely the way of life and the liberties they enjoy today".

For a long time, there was no statue of Dowding to celebrate his leadership during the battle, but in October 1988 one was finally unveiled by Queen Elizabeth, the Queen Mother, patron of the Fighter Association, outside the RAF church of St Clement Danes on London's Strand. Other memorials have followed. At Capel-le-Ferne in Kent stands the Battle of Britain National Memorial, opened in July 1993. Another Battle of Britain memorial was erected near Croydon airport in 1991, site of many attacks during the battle itself. In 2005, a major monument was set up on the Victoria Embankment in central London.

The many Fighter Command stations from which the battle was fought have fared unevenly in the post-war years. Biggin Hill and Kenley retained a few buildings from the war period, but the best preserved air station was at Duxford, which became home to the Imperial War Museum's aircraft collection. The Uxbridge control centre for 11 Group has also been preserved and restored in its entirety. Bentley Priory was until recently still home to a number of different RAF and Ministry of Defence departments, including the Air Historical Branch.

The Battle of Britain has become one of the central legends of Britain's war effort. It has benefited from the persistent image of an English David taking on a German Goliath. Its enduring quality stems directly from the historical circumstances which made it a necessary victory. The threat of invasion against the only country in Europe still fighting against German domination of the Continent gave the battle the same iconic status accorded to the defeat of the Spanish Armada or the victory at Waterloo. The battle was also fought and won by a handful of young men rather than whole armies. The image of the "few", even if it exaggerates the extent of the disparity between the two sides, resonates with the idea of lonely defiance against tyranny. Though the Battle of Britain did not win the war, it kept alive the prospect of final victory.

THE BATTLE OF BRITAIN MONUMENT, LONDON

The Battle of Britain Monument stands on London's Victoria Embankment not far from the Houses of Parliament. It was formally opened in September 2005 in front of 70 pilot veterans from the battle and was the result of collaboration between the Battle of Britain Historical Society and Westminster Council. The monument site granted by the Council was a 25-metre (82-foot) granite structure which had originally been built as a smoke outlet for steam-powered underground trains. A walkway was cut through the structure, and bronze panels depicting the battle and Britain at war in 1940 attached on either side. A full list of those who fought in the battle is included, organized by nationality. The monument was sculpted by Paul Day who flew in a Battle of Britain flight aircraft as part of his research into the experience of fighting in the air in 1940.

INDEX

page references in italics refer to pictures

TRANSLATION   CREDITS

Item 3
The German army order of 17 July 1940 for the onset of preparations for an attack against southern England. The original plan envisaged three main attack groups based around Calais, Le Havre and Cherbourg for attacks between Weymouth and Margate.

(Issued by HQ OKH (Supreme Command of the German Army), 17.7.40.)

The Führer has ordered preparations for the attack on England.

The preparations will take place on the principle:

That one Calais (A.O.K. 16) attack wing is deployed from the Ostend–mouth of the Somme area against the enemy coast between Margate and Hastings.

One Le Havre (A.O.K. 9) attack wing is deployed from the Dieppe–Caen area against the enemy coast between Brighton and Portsmouth.

One Cherbourg (A.O.K. 6) attack wing is deployed from the area around Cherbourg against the enemy coast, both sides of Weymouth.

More details follow on this.

As a lead-up to the organisation of the attack, the following is ordered:

1.) Organisation of command:

a) 6th Army (without Gen. Command X with 57 and 223 Inf. Div.) falls under the command of Army Group B.

New dividing line between Army Group A and Army Group B: Port en Bessin (33 km north west of Caen) – Bayeux – Condé (Group A towns) – Alençon (Group B town) – North east border of the Sarthe Département.

b) Within Army Group A, A.O.K. 9 takes over the section on both sides of the Seine.

Proposal for a new dividing line between A.O.K. 16 and A.O.K. 9 is to be submitted by Army Group A.

c) Take-over of command is to take place as soon as possible.

Army Group B shall report after agreement with Army Group A, when take-over can take place.

2.) Assignment of forces:

The following are to assemble for deployment in the first attack strikes:

a) under A.O.K. 16 in the area Bruges – Mouth of the Somme:

Gen. Command VII with 7th and 1st Mountain Div.

Gen. Command XIII with 17th and 35th Infantry Division

Gen. Command XXXVIII with 26th and 34th Infantry Division

b) under A.O.K. 9 in the area of Dieppe – Caen:

Gen. Command VIII with 8th and 28th Infantry Divsiion

Gen. Command X with 30th and 6th Mountain Division

c) under A.O.K. 6 in the Area of Cherbourg – Granville – Isigny:

Gen. Command II with 12th, 31st and 32nd Infantry Div.

These are to be distributed over the area in a way that on the one hand enables training for the tasks ahead and on the other hand facilitates subsequent supplies into the drop zones. They are not to be deployed in the front line defending the coast.

The sections to be supplied by train are indicated in Annex 1. The units not listed here are to be brought in by overland march by the army groups. The units designated for the parade in Paris will not be transferred until after the parade. The units will fall under the command of the appropriate army once they arrive at their new army section.

d) The areas left free by the bringing in of units in accordance with points a)–c) are to be taken over by other divisions after more detailed discussion and agreement between the army groups. The aim here should be distribution in accordance with territorial demands (supervision, harvests, salvaging of captured goods etc.).

e) The army troops included in the groups of forces referred to in a) – c) and the deployment of army artillery on the Channel coast under the command of the Supreme Commander of the Navy will be the subject of separate orders. The transfer of army troops ordered on 12.7.40, by O.K.H. Gen. Staff of the Army Op. Dept (III) No. 385/40 g.Cd., is to continue as planned.

3.) Timing:

Transfers to be carried out in accordance with point 2) must have taken place at the latest by 31.7.

4.) Reporting:

The army groups shall report immediately to O.K.H. Gen Staff of the Army Op. Dept. the intended division of their armies and the new headquarters of the 9th Army on the basis of this order.

Signed: Halder

Annex 1: Summary of transports (lists the transport unit, where and at what time loading should begin and end, where they should unload and then where higher staff personel should join to immediately load).

Translator's note:
A.O.K. = Army High Command
O.K.H. = Army Supreme Command

The publisher would like to thank the following people for their help with the production of this book:

Olivia Smales, IMG
Squadron Leader Stuart Balfour, Royal Air Force
Peter Elliott, Nina Burls and Rebecca Dalley, Royal Air Force Museum
Mary Hudson, Royal Air Force Historical Branch
Hugh Alexander, The National Archives, Kew
Shaheeda Sabir, Curtis Brown
Gill Coleridge and Cara Jones, Rogers, Coleridge and White

PHOTOGRAPHS

The vast majority of photographs reproduced in this book have been taken from the collections of the Photograph Archive at the RAF Air Historical Branch. Reference numbers for each of the photographs is indicated below, giving the page on which they appear in the book and location indicator.

Key: t = top, b = bottom, l = left, r = right and c = centre.

RAF Air Historical Branch (UK Crown Copyright. Reproduced with permission of the Controller, HMSO, London.): front endpapers, 2, 4, 5, 6t, 6r, 6bl, 6bc, 8tl, 8tr, 9tr, 10l, 10bc, 10tr, 11tc, 11tr, 11br, 12bl, 15br, 23bl, 23tr, 24l, 24tr, 24cr, 24bc, 26bl, 26tr, 27bl, 27cr, 28c, 30bl, 31c, 31r, 32bc, 33cl, 33bc, 34tr, 36bl, 36tr, 36cr, 37c, 38bl, 38br, 39c, 39tr, 40bl, 40bc, 40br, 40tr, 41tr, 42tl, 42bc, 42rc, 43c, 43tr, 43b, 44bc, 48br, 50tr, 51c, 51tc, 53cr, 54tr, 60c, 61tr, 61cl, back endpapers.

Photographs from sources outside the RAF Air Historical Branch, with the kind permission of the following:

AKG-Images: 48r; **Alamy:** /Simon Hadley: 61br; **Aviation-images.com:** 20cr; © **Barry Duffield:** 60bc; **Carlton Books:** /Steve Behan: 61tl, 61bc; **Corbis:** 14bc, 15c, 40bc; /Bettmann: 16cr, 35br, 50bc, 54br, 57cl; /Hulton-Deutsch Collection: 44lc, 45c; /Underwood & Underwood: 34c; **Getty Images:** 7tl, 7tr, 8r, 9bc, 13bc, 15tl, 17l, 17bc, 18tr, 21r, 29cl, 29bc, 29tr, 30tr, 34bc, 34tr, 42c, 45tr, 52bc, 52tr, 54bl, 55cl, 56bc, 56tr, 57bc, 58cl, 58br; /Popperfoto: 44tr, 49c, 49cl, 55br, 58tr; /Time & Life Pictures: 18br, 41bl, 48bc, 54tc; **Imperial War Museums:** 1 (CH 00070), 5r (PST 14972), 14l (CH 010270), 16bl (HU 002280), 20l (CH 003517), 21l (D 12125), 22c (C 001868), 23br (HU 042365), 24br (CH 001887), 28bl (CH 010253), 28br (PST 003096), 31tc (CH 000740), 33tr (CH 003193), 34bc (H 003512), 50bl (CH 1388), 52bl (H 004062), 53tr (PST 2916), 56bl (PST 3447), 59cr (PST 14972); **The Kobal Collection:** United Artists: 60r; **Mirrorpix.com:** 7bc, 9bl, 18tr, 19c, 20br, 32r, 49tr, 59bc; **The News, Portsmouth:** 19bc; **Press Association Images:** AP: 37tl; **Private Collection:** 11c, 25tl, 55tr; **Rex Features:** 27br; **Royal Air Force, HMSO:** 31cl; **Scala:** BPK: 12bc, 13tr, 26bc, 34bl, 53bc, 53c; /Bayerische Staatbibliothe: 37cr, 37bc, 38c, 39bc; /Atelier Bieber/Nather: 32tl; /Arthur Grimm: 13bc, 27tl; /Herbert Hoffmann: 32c; /Hans Hubmann: 13tl; /Benno Wundshammer: 12tc; **Topfoto.co.uk:** 14tr, 22tr, 25tr, 29bl, 30br, 57tr; /Alinari: 51tr; /The Granger Collection: 44bl; /Ullsteinbild: 15tr, 16tr, 17bl, 18bl, 22bc, 25c, 37cl, 45cr, 45tc, 48c.

Every effort has been made to acknowledge correctly and contact the source and/or copyright holder of each picture, and Carlton Books apologizes for any unintentional errors or omissions, which will be corrected in future editions of this book.

MEMORABILIA

With kind permission of:

The Royal Air Force Museum (UK Crown Copyright. Reproduced with permission of the Controller, HMSO, London.): Item 1, Item 6, Item 7, Item 9, Item 14, Item 15.

The Royal Air Force Museum: Item 2, Item 11, Item 13, Item 18, Item 19, Item 20.

The National Archives, Kew: Item 4, Item 5, Item 8, Item 10, Item 16, Item 17.

Curtis Brown Ltd, London, on behalf of the Estate of Winston Churchill. © **Winston S. Churchill.** (With thanks also to the Churchill Archives Centre, Cambridge.): Item 12.

FURTHER INFORMATION

Royal Air Force: www.raf.mod.uk
Royal Air Force Air Historical Branch: www.raf.mod.uk/ahb/
Royal Air Force Museum: www.rafmuseum.org.uk
The National Archives, Kew: www.nationalarchives.gov.uk/
The Churchill Archives Centre, Cambridge: www.chu.cam.ac.uk/archives/